ANCIENT WISDOM

40 ILLUSTRATIONS FROM THE ANCIENT WISDOM ORACLE DECK

BY TIFFANY TOLAND-SCOTT

A TIFFANY'S REALM™ PUBLICATION

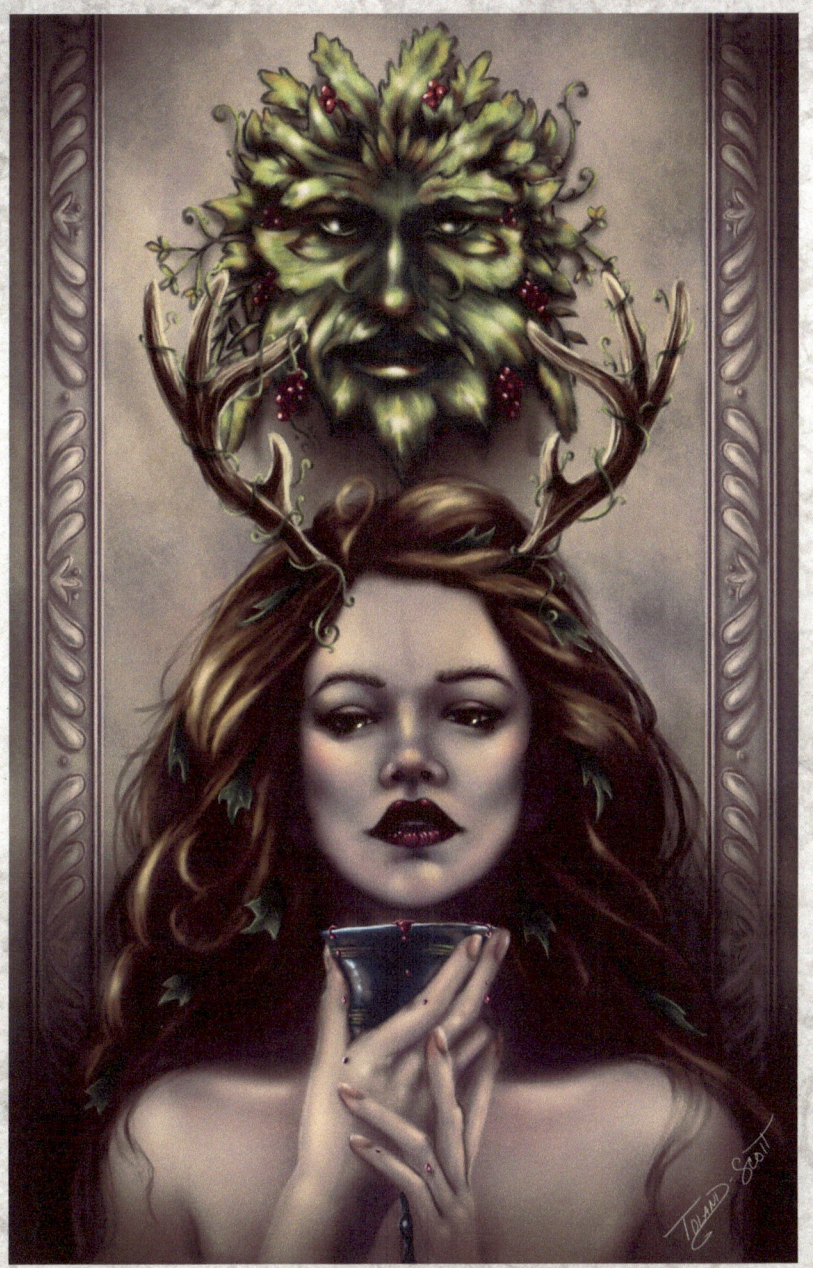

ABUNDANCE - In the oracle deck, "Abundance" represents Earth. I've often drawn this horned woman, who is in my mind the protector or goddess of the forest. She appears in the deck twice, the second time representing The Divine. The Green Man behind her and goblet of wine in her hand represent our ties to the Earth and nature, and are symbolic of the meaning of this card: Slow down, enjoy your home life, and indulge a little bit.

This piece was painted digitally in 2011.

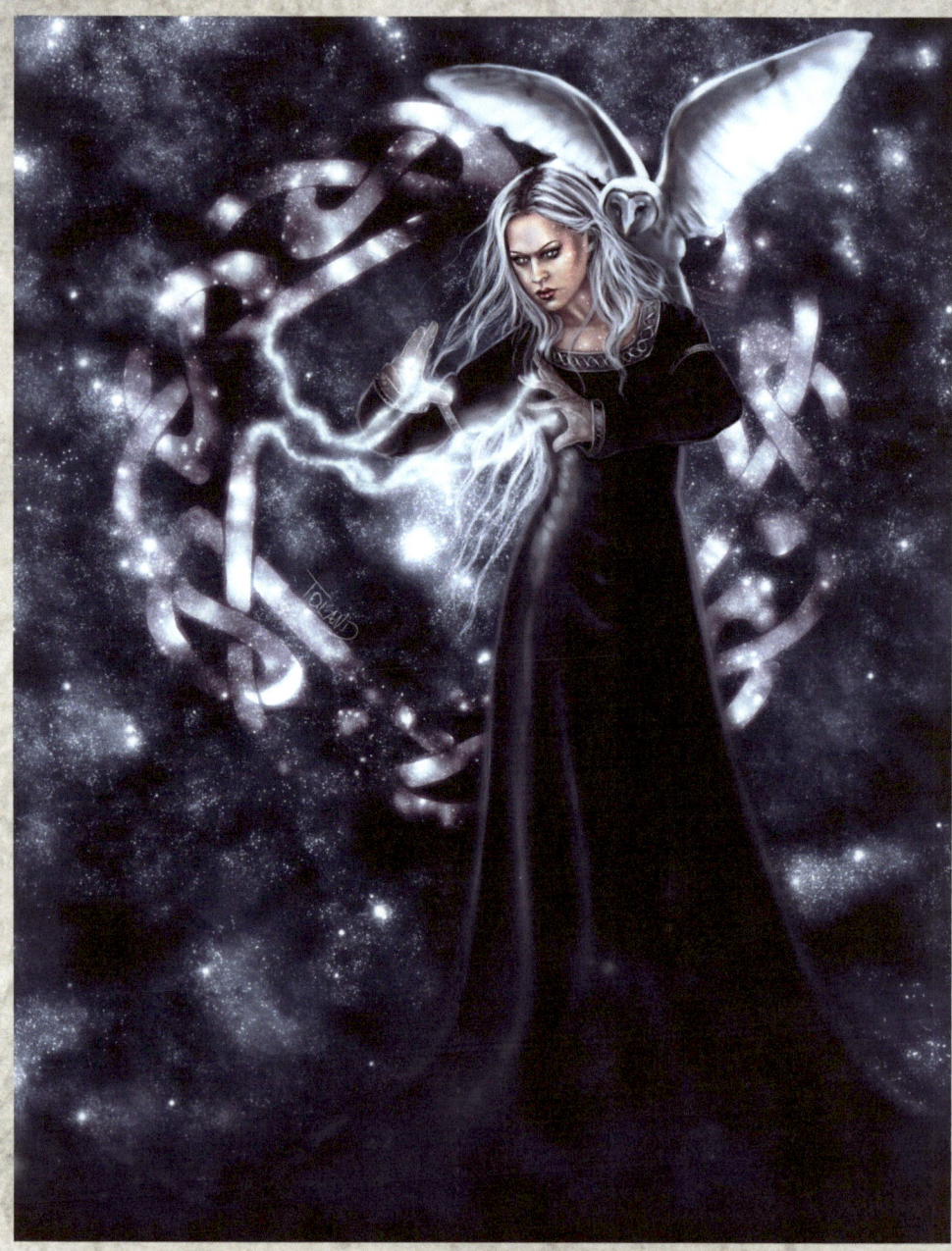

ARIANRHOD - Arianrhod originates in Welsh mythology and is the Goddess of the silver wheel. Her symbols includes owls, stars, the night sky, and silver wheels. She is also associated with fertility and creation, and for this reason she represents Fertility in the oracle deck. I've depicted her weaving stars into her silver wheel, a reminder that fertility is not always tied to reproduction and can be indicative of having a lot of creative ideas as well.

This was painted digitally in 2010.

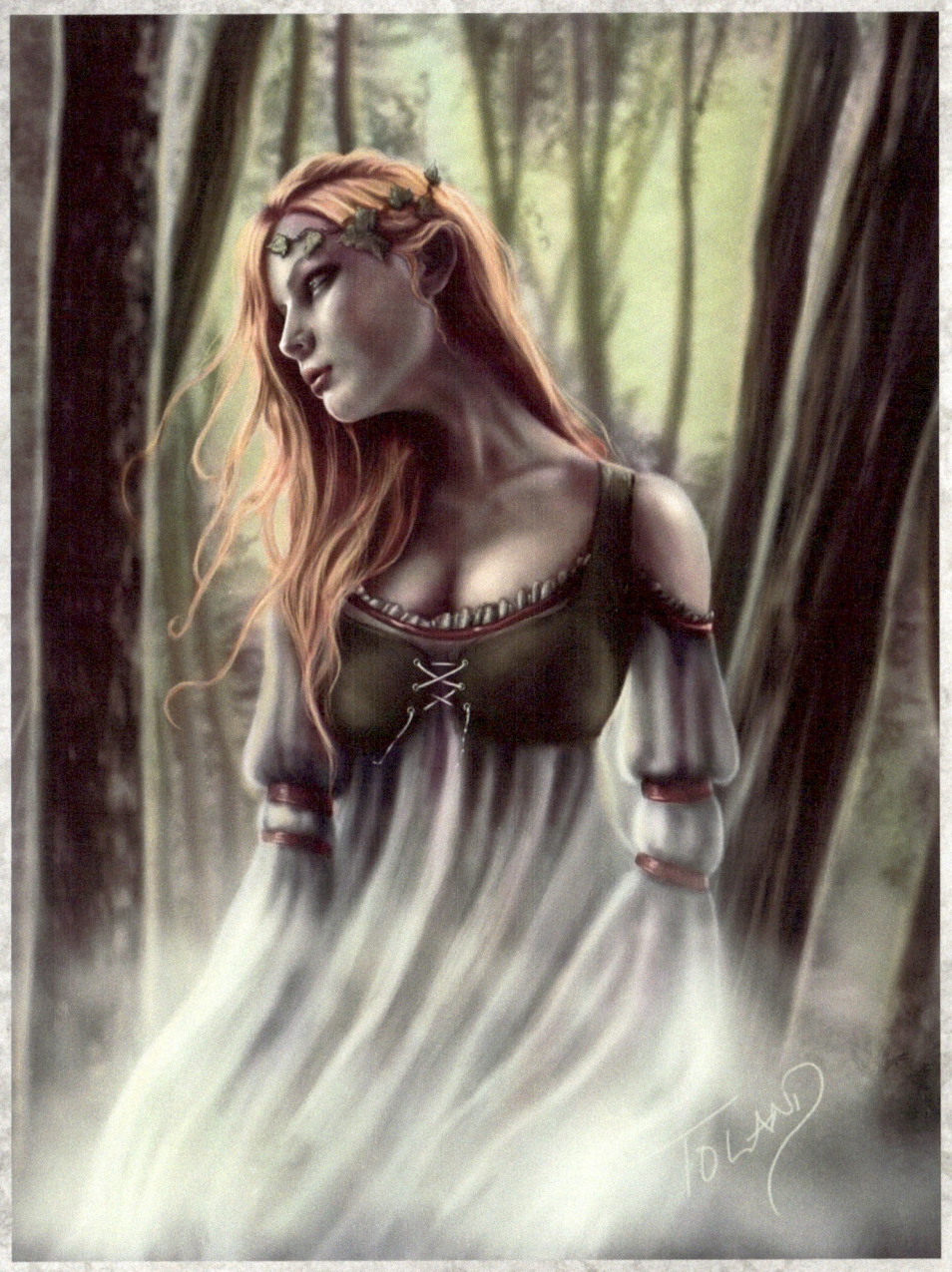

BENEATH THE IVY - This solitary ghostly woman represents Mind in the
oracle deck. To me she seems lost in thought, perfect for the introspective
properties of this card. The painting itself is something pulled from my own
imagination, inspired by a brief passage in one of my favorite books.

This was painted digitally in 2010.

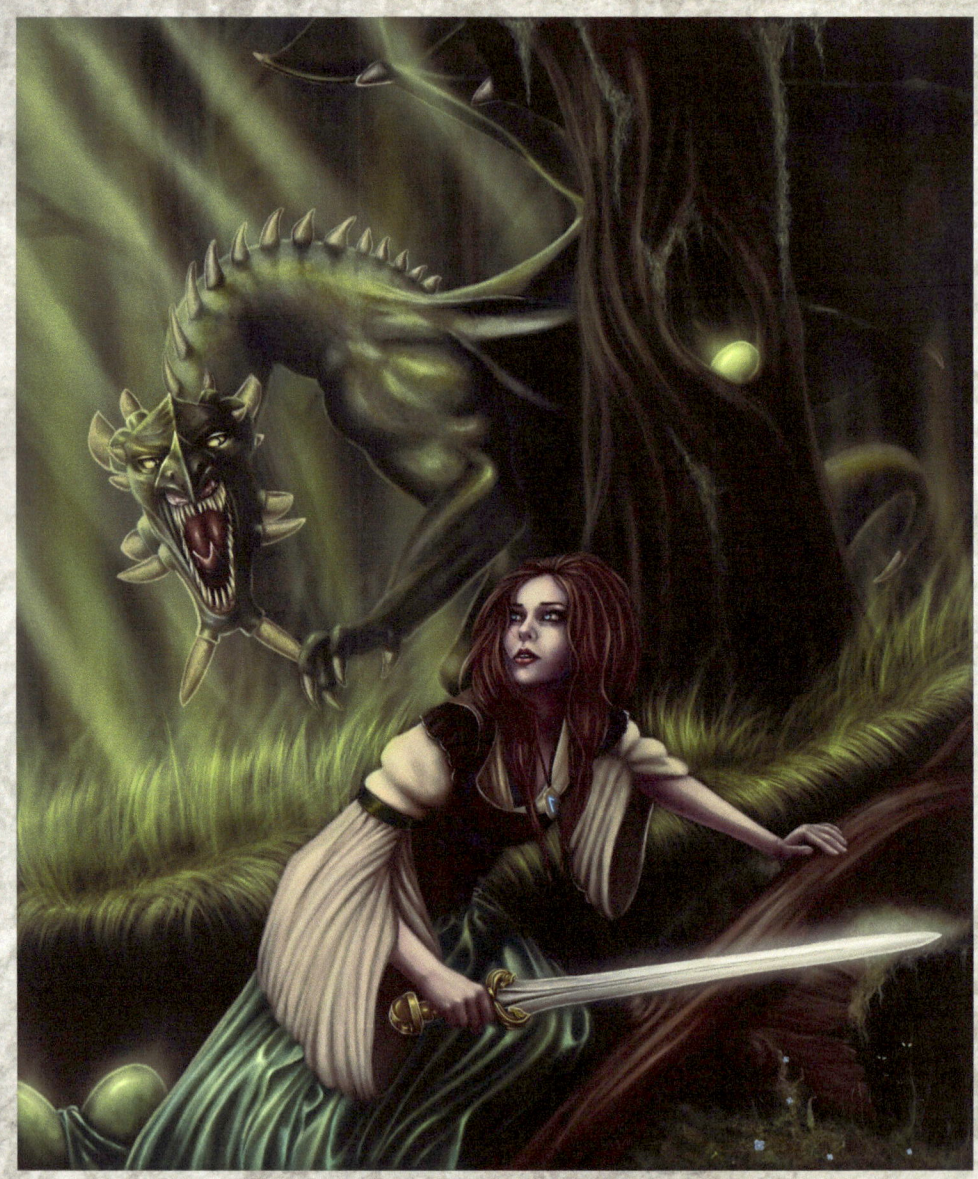

BEWARE THE WOODS - As a child I spent most of my afternoons playing in the woods surrounding my family's home. The Wenatchee National Forest is dense and dark every season of the year, and rumors of haunted grottos and mysterious monsters abound in the tiny ghost town where I lived. My imagination ran wild there, and I battled dragons and sorcerers and fled from invading armies in the shade of the evergreens. This card represents determination.

This was painted digitally in 2009.

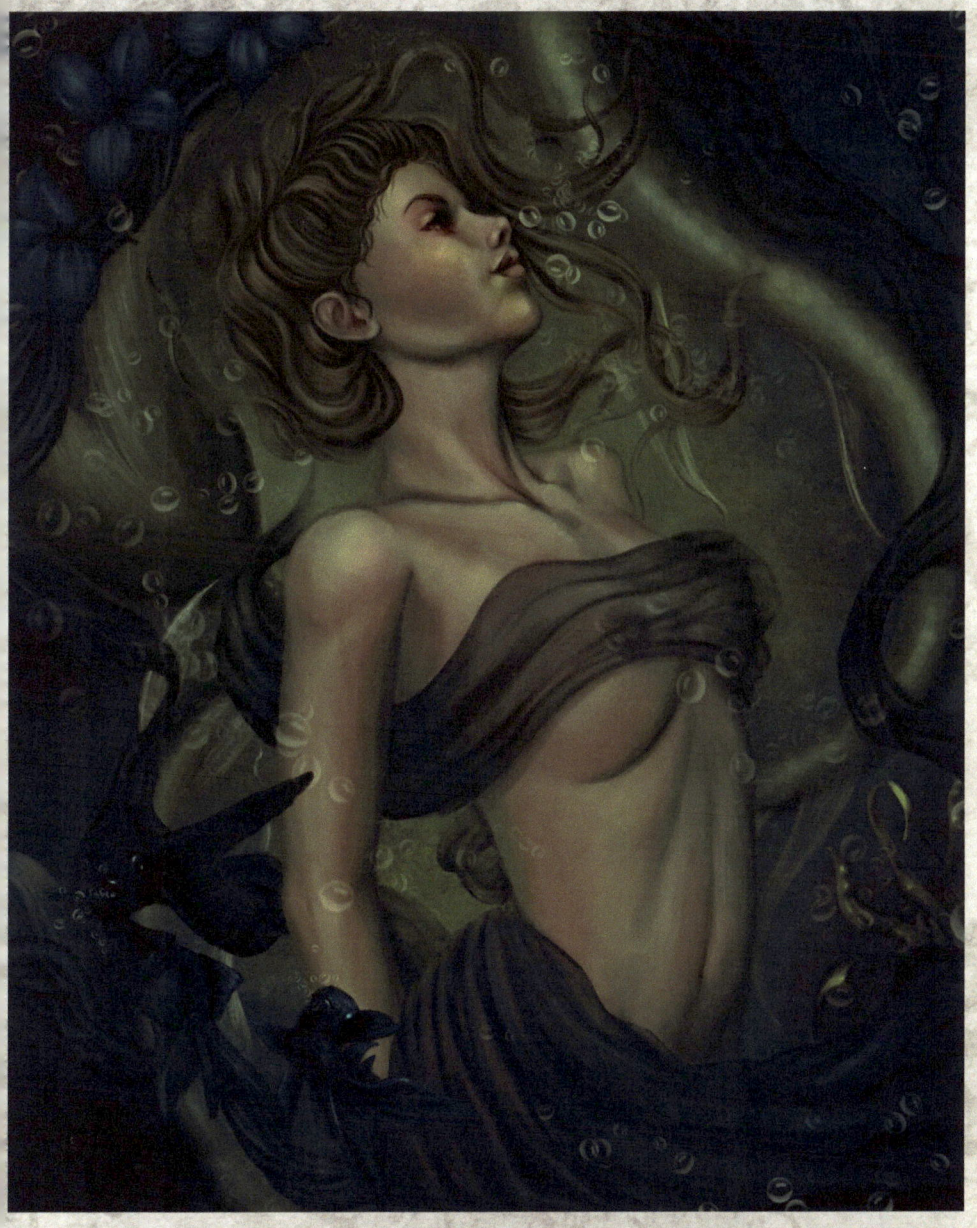

BIRTH OF A SIREN - Stories of sirens dragging men and young women to their drowning deaths are found throughout mythologies worldwide. Often these stories are tragic, but every so often one comes along about a young woman freed from an unwanted life by the transformative properties of water. This painting of one such maiden seemed a perfect fit for The Sun.

This was painted digitally in 2013.

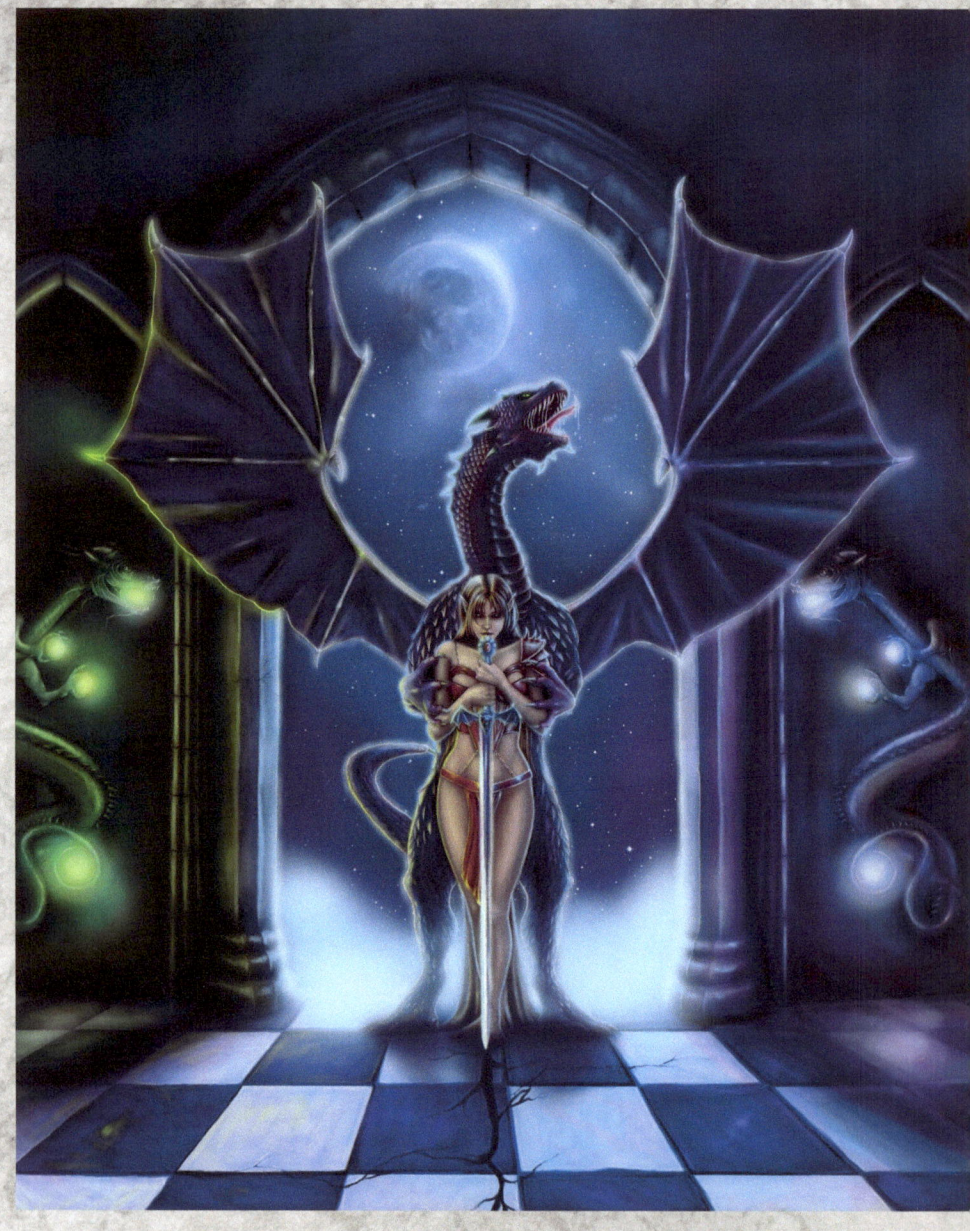

BLOOD PACT - This card represents justice and cause and effect. Our actions are bigger than just ourselves. They effect everyone and everything around us, and sometimes more than we can see.

This was painted digitally in 2009.

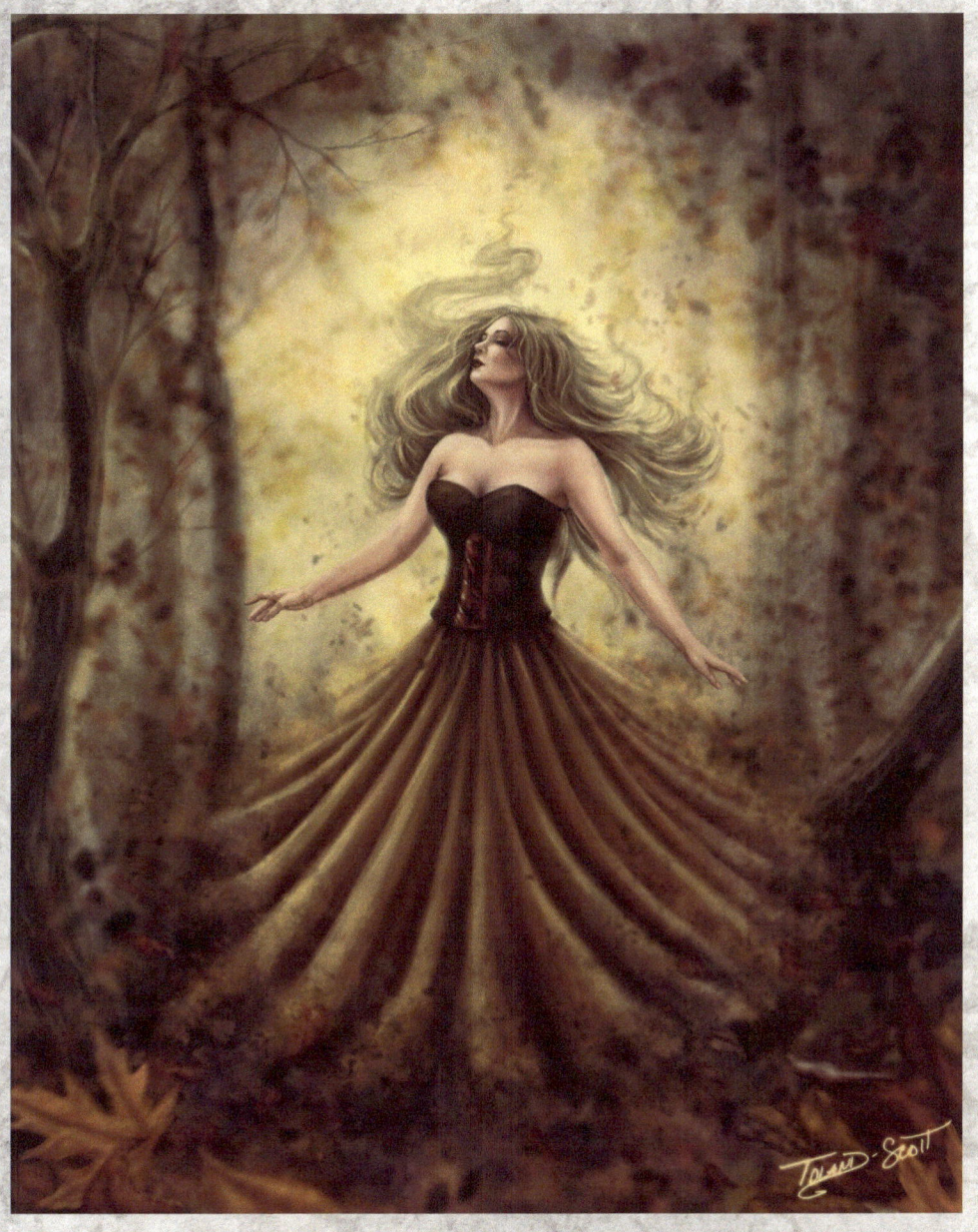

BREATH OF AUTUMN - Autumn might be my favorite season, and it's
not just because it's the season of my birthday! I love the firey autumn colors
and the refreshing crispness of the autumn air. This card represents Fire in the
oracle deck, and reminds us not to get too swept up in our passions. Fire is
beneficial, but it can also be destructive.

This was painted digitally in 2012.

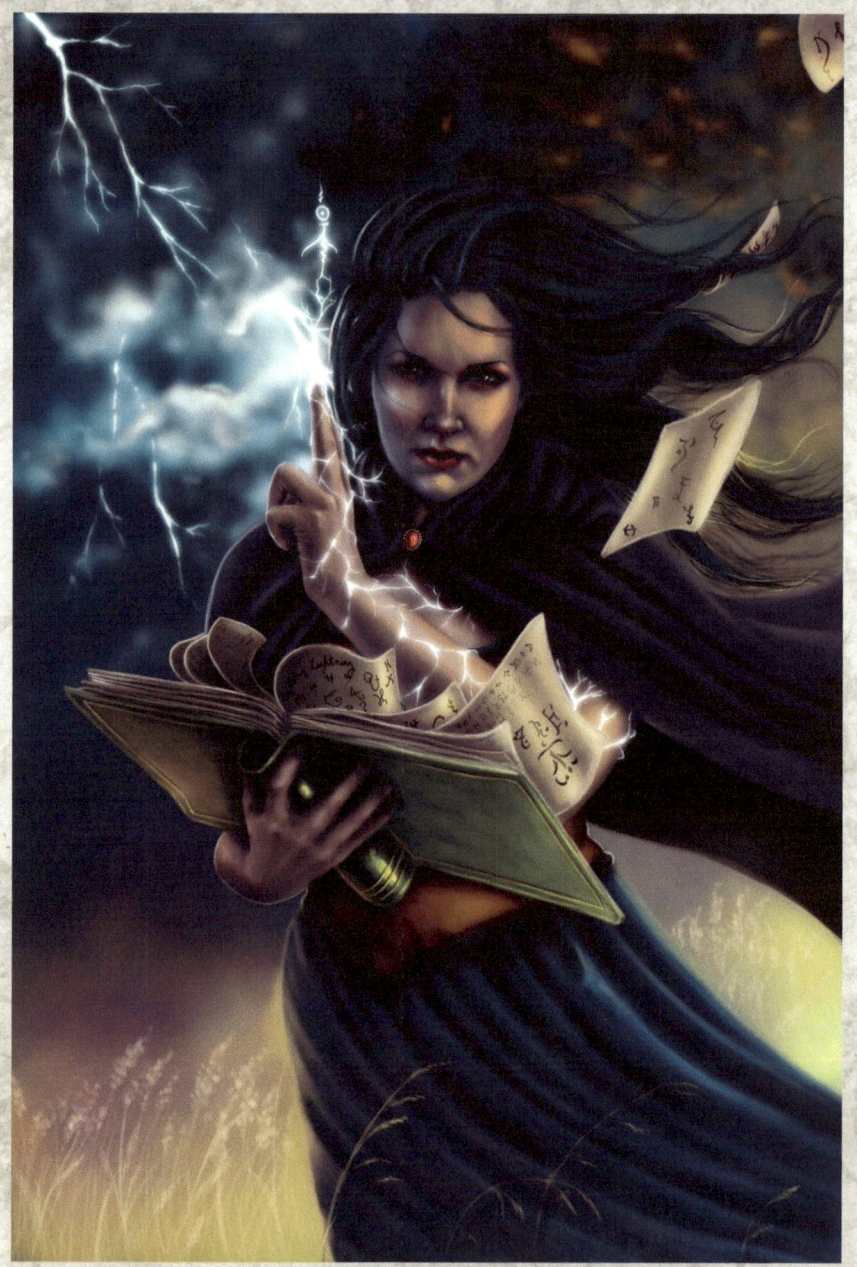

CALLING THE STORM - I have an uncanny ability to predict the weather with my paintings, it seems. The morning I painted this one turned into an afternoon where I was plagued by thunderstorms and forced to shut down my equipment over and over again. This card seemed a natural fit for The Magician, thanks both to the sorceress depicted here and the strange circumstances of this painting's creation.

This was painted digitally in 2010.

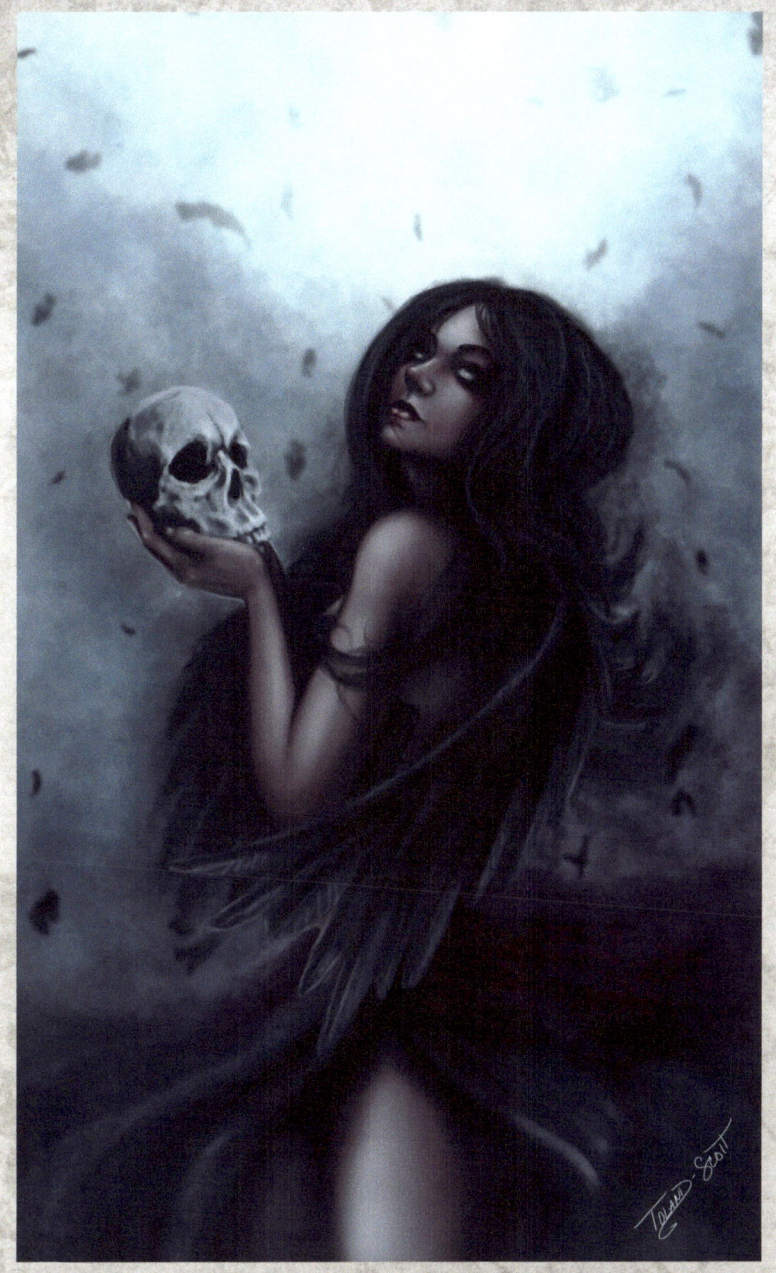

CALL OF THE MORRIGHAN - Known as a Celtic war goddess, she was in charge of deciding which warriors would walk off the field of battle. Often appearing as a crow or raven or accompanied by a murder of crows, she is also believed to collect the souls of warriors from the battle field and take them to the underworld.

This was painted digitally in 2012.

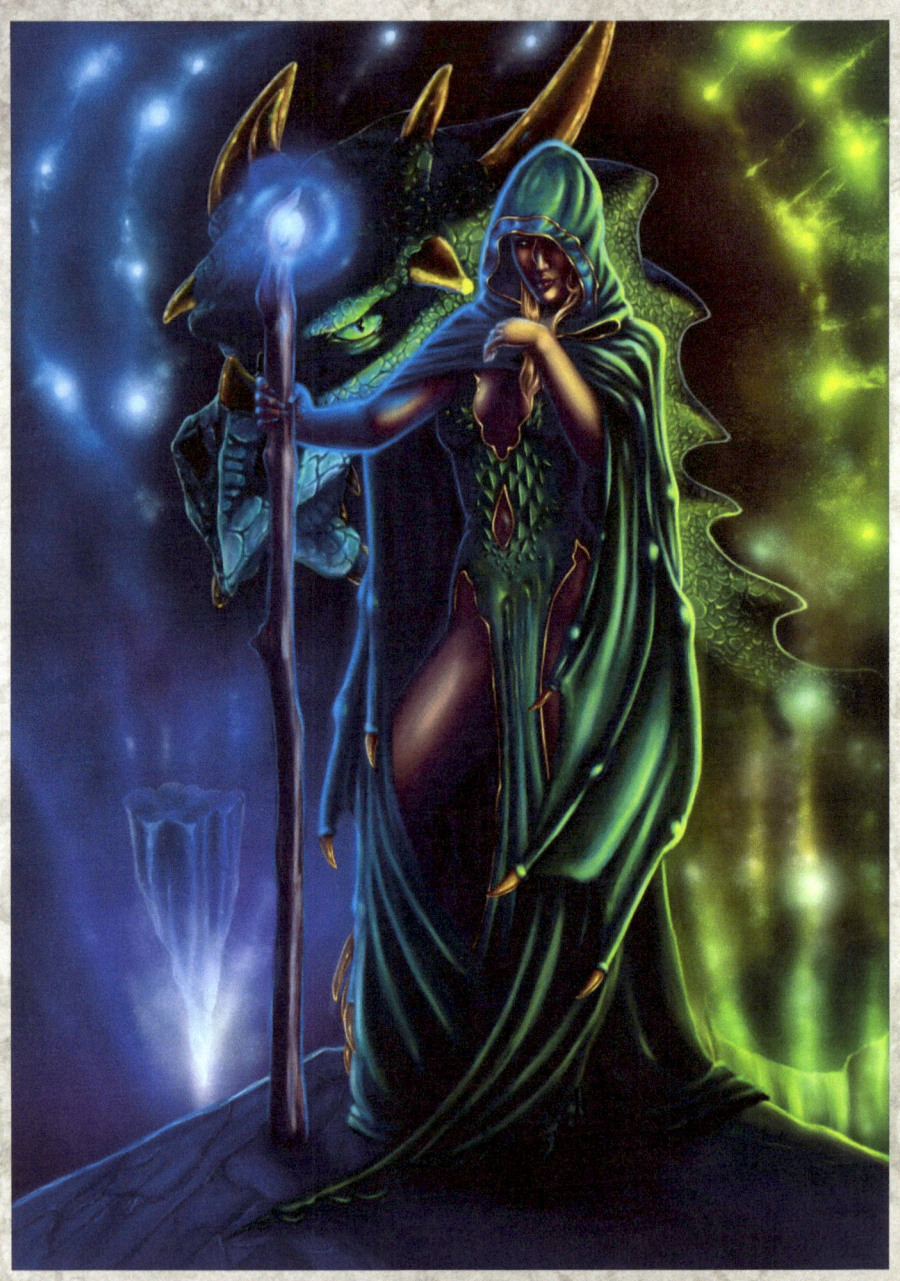

DRAGON'S BANE - Dragons are often thought of as horrid nightmare beasts that destroy villages and eat virgins, but frequently in mythology they are noble, cunning, and wise. These two represent Honesty in the oracle deck, and what better to keep you honest than one fierce dragon and a powerful witch?

This was painted digitally in 2009.

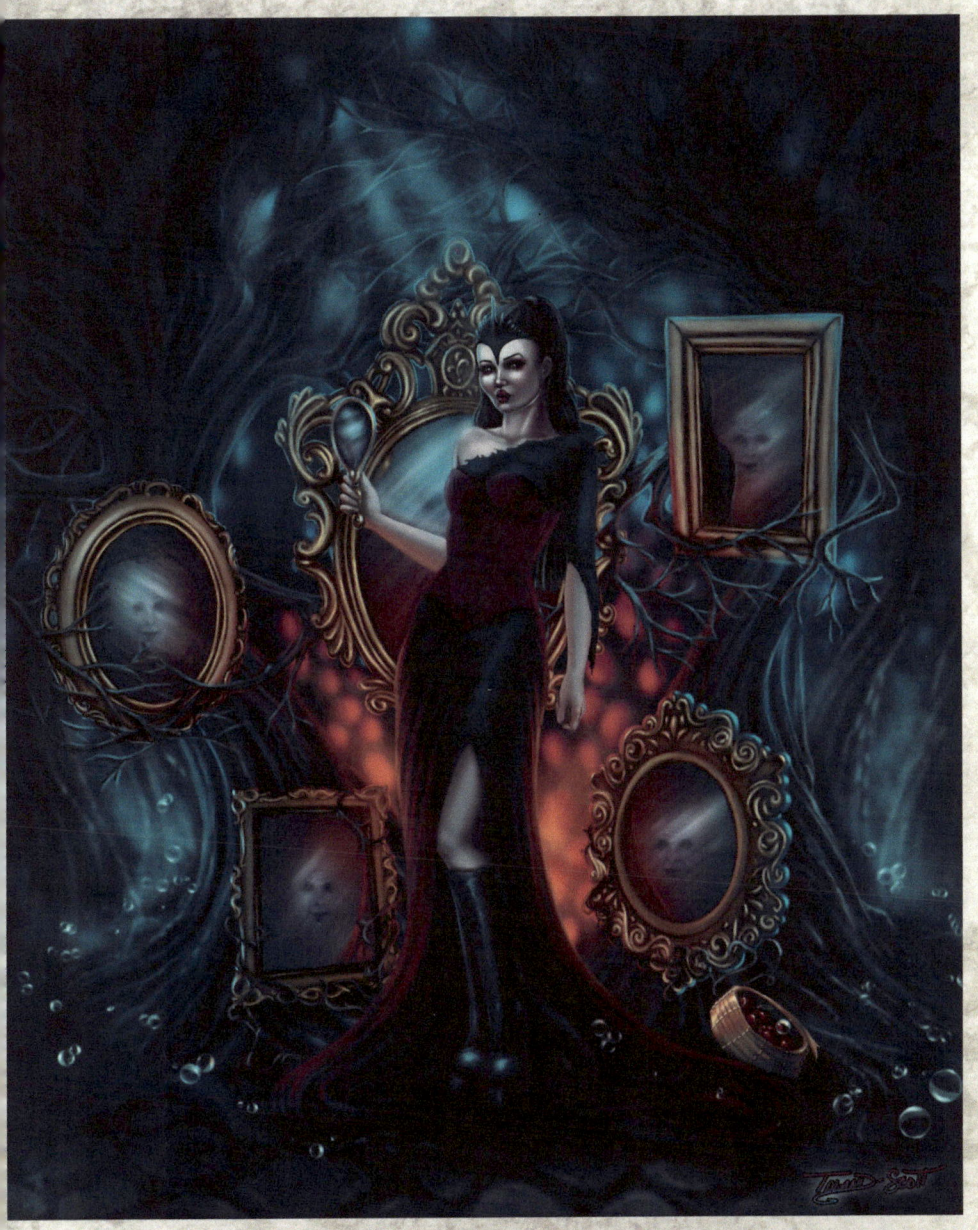

EVIL QUEEN COMPLEX - I just love evil queens and wicked stepmothers. I never have enough opportunities to paint them. Maybe it's just fun to be bad, but they always seem like the most interesting characters to me. This painting represents The Crossroads in the oracle deck, the mirrors reminding us to reflect on the path we've traveled so far.

This was painted digitally in 2012.

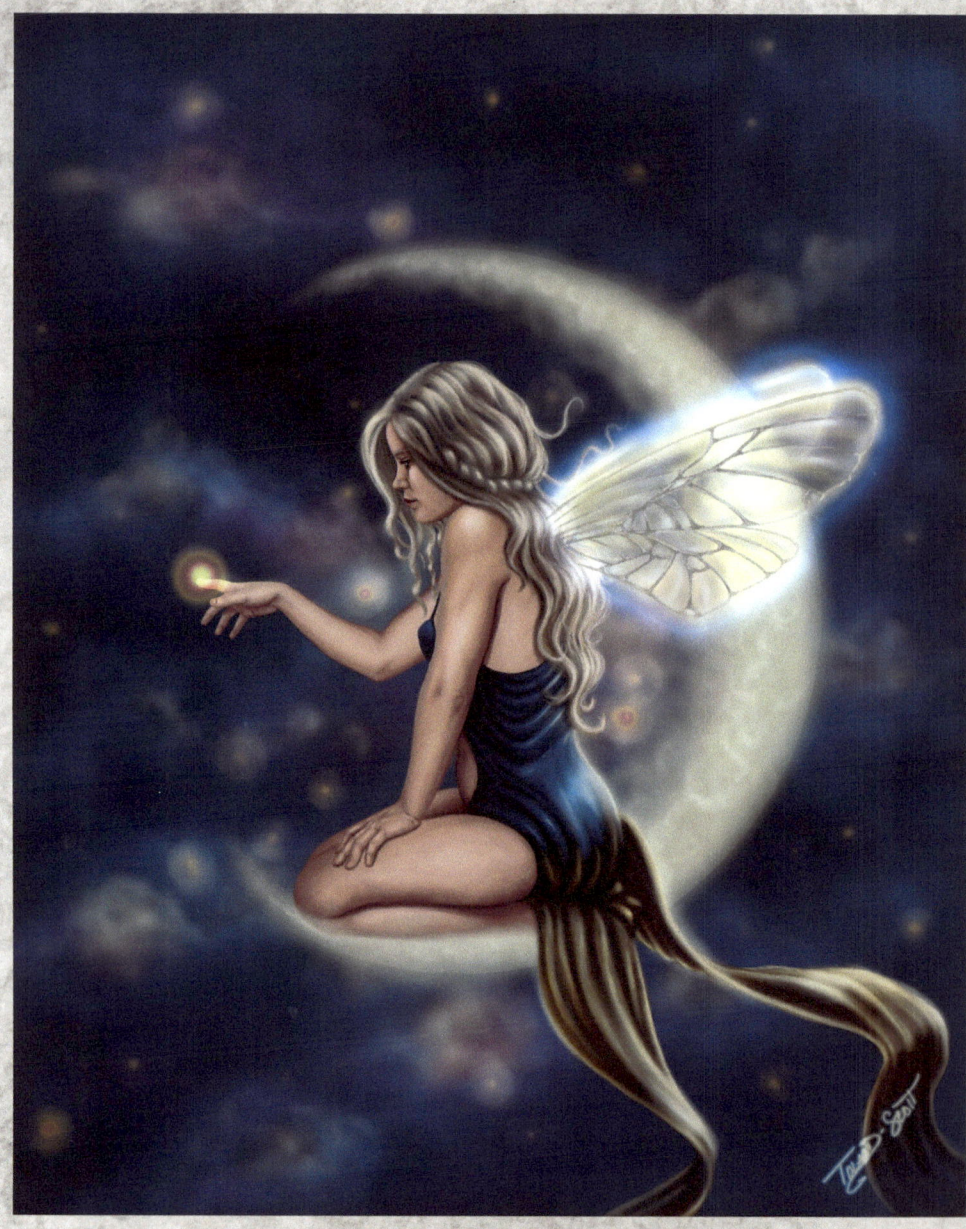

FIREFLY MOON - This sweet faerie is perched on the crescent moon, and a firefly balances on the tip of her finger. This card represents Compassion, and reminds us to be gentle with those who are smaller or weaker than ourselves.

This was painted digitally in 2012.

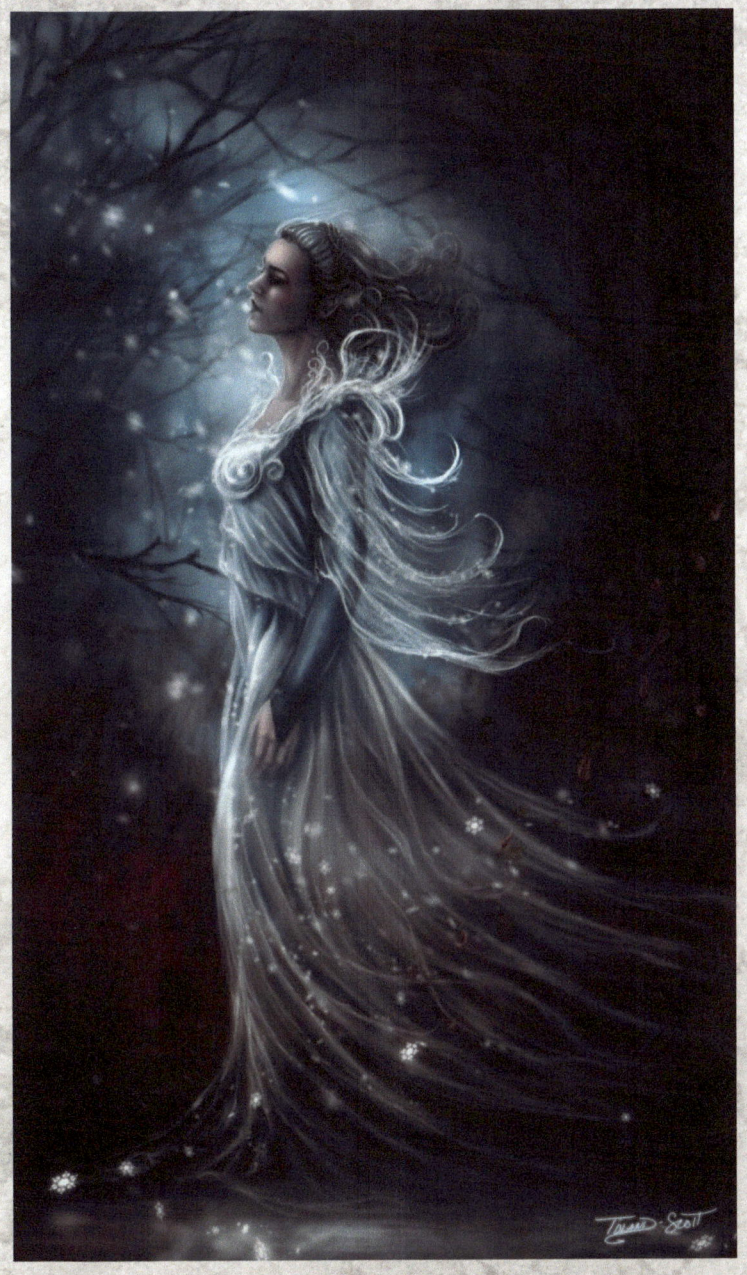

FIRST KISS OF FROST - I tried to capture the transition from autumn to winter in this painting. Snowflakes and autumn leaves swirl around the misty figure somewhere deep in the woods. This card represents Choice in the oracle deck, and is symbolic of the struggle many people face to either move forward, or backward.

This was painted digitally in 2012.

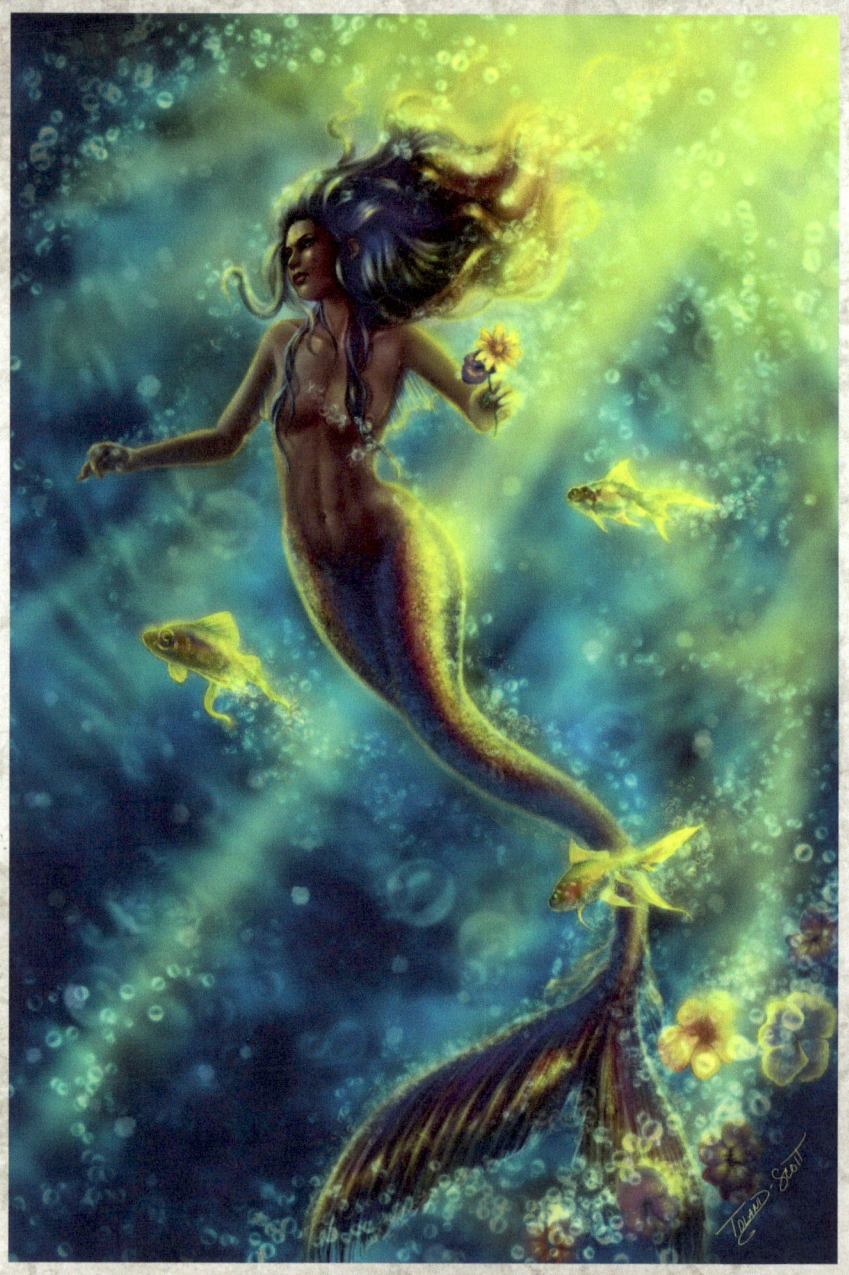

FORBIDDEN DESIRE - This painting was inspired by the hidden language of flowers. A pansy and honeyflower together symbolize forbidden love. I imagine some landlubber has fallen hard for this mermaid and has left her these flowers.

This was painted digitally in 2013.

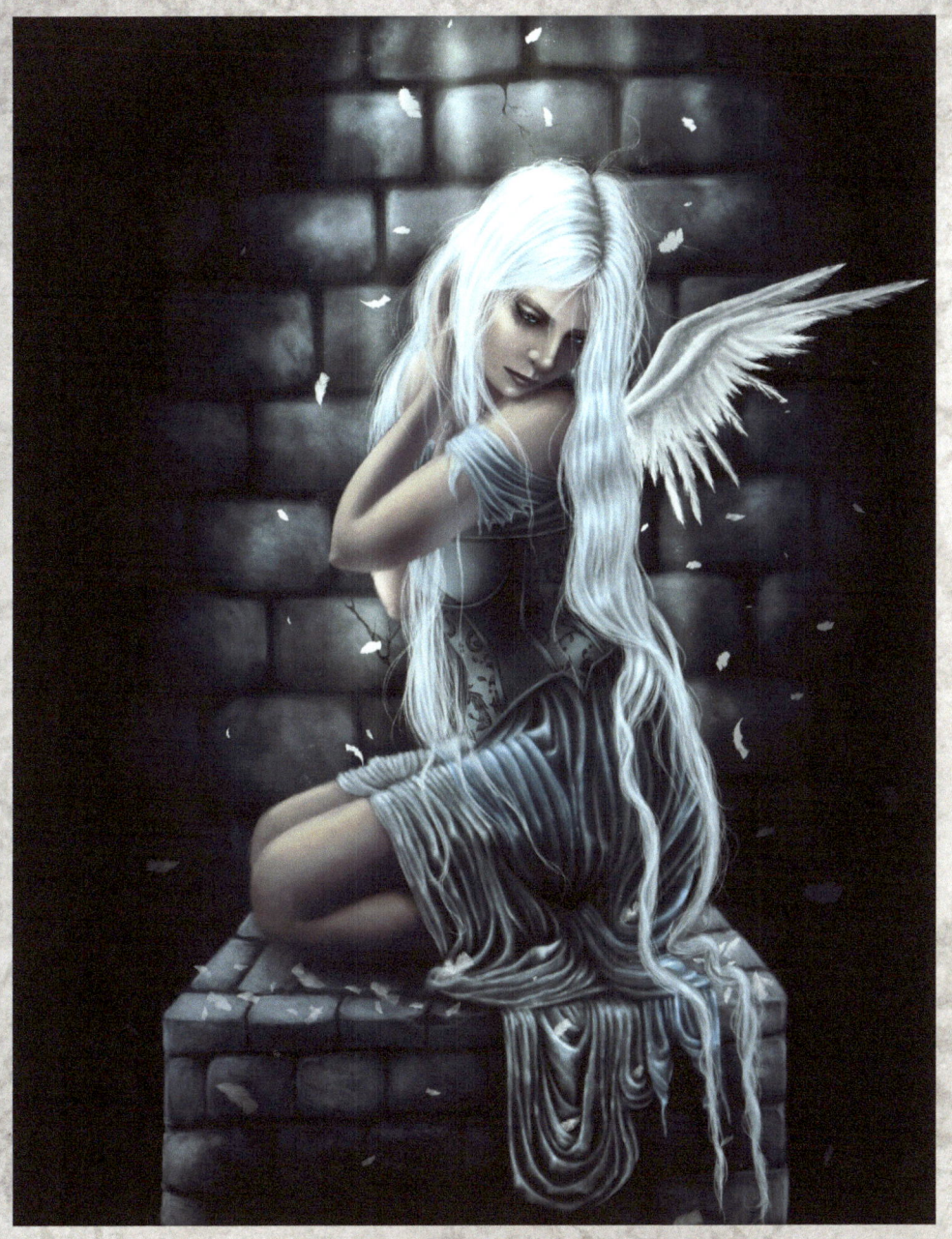

FORGOTTEN - One part of a set of paintings, this angel is trapped inside an oubliette. She seemed like a natural fit for The Tower, a card representing upheaval.

This was painted digitally in 2008.

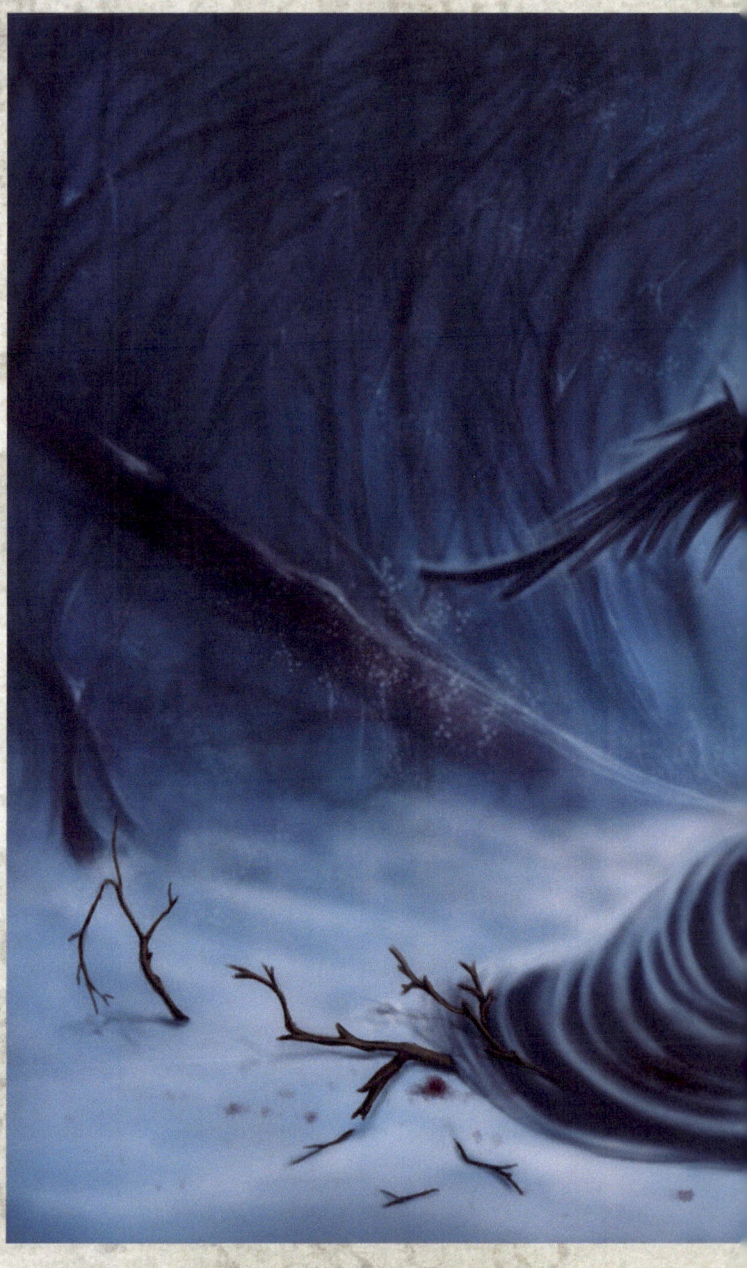

LAST OF MY INNOCENCE - This fallen angel clutches her last white
feather, the last little bit of her innocence. She represents the Judgment card in
the oracle deck, a reminder to accept and embrace our past as part of ourselves.

This was painted digitally in 2012.

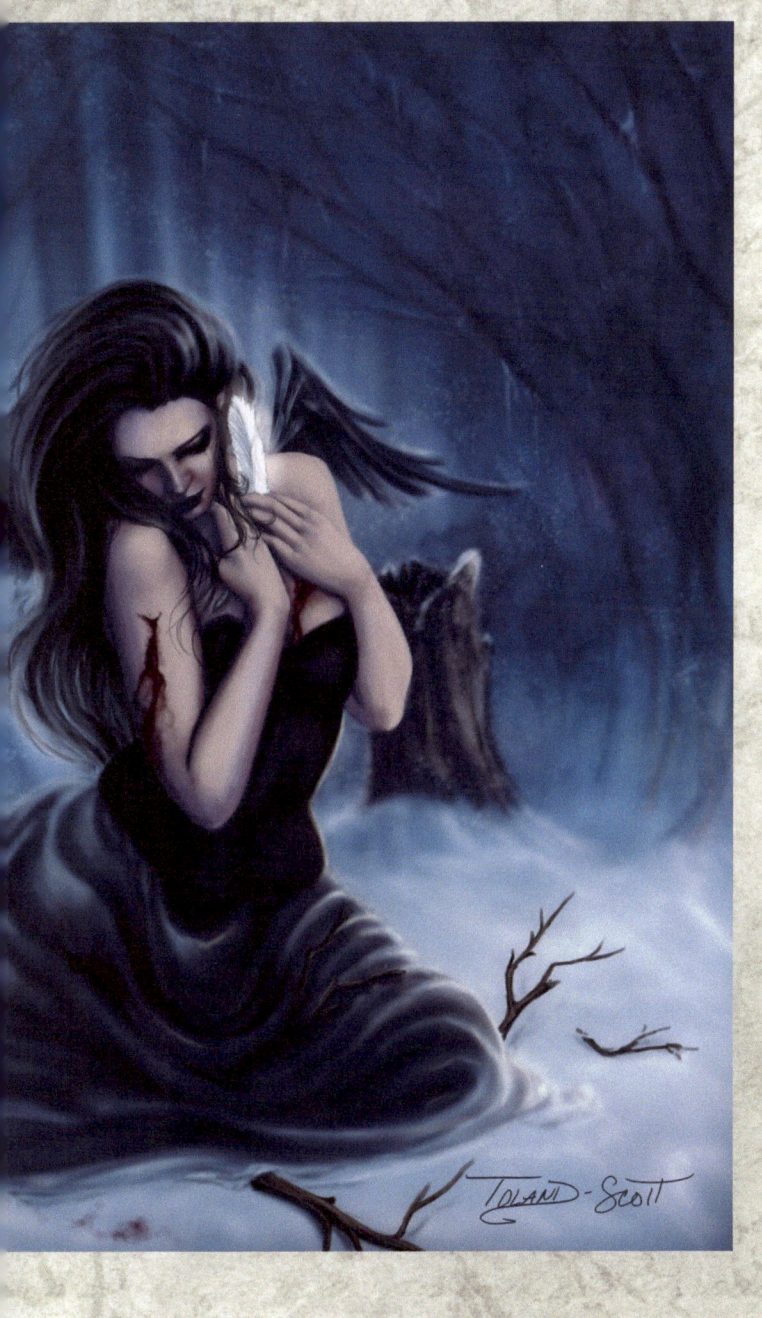

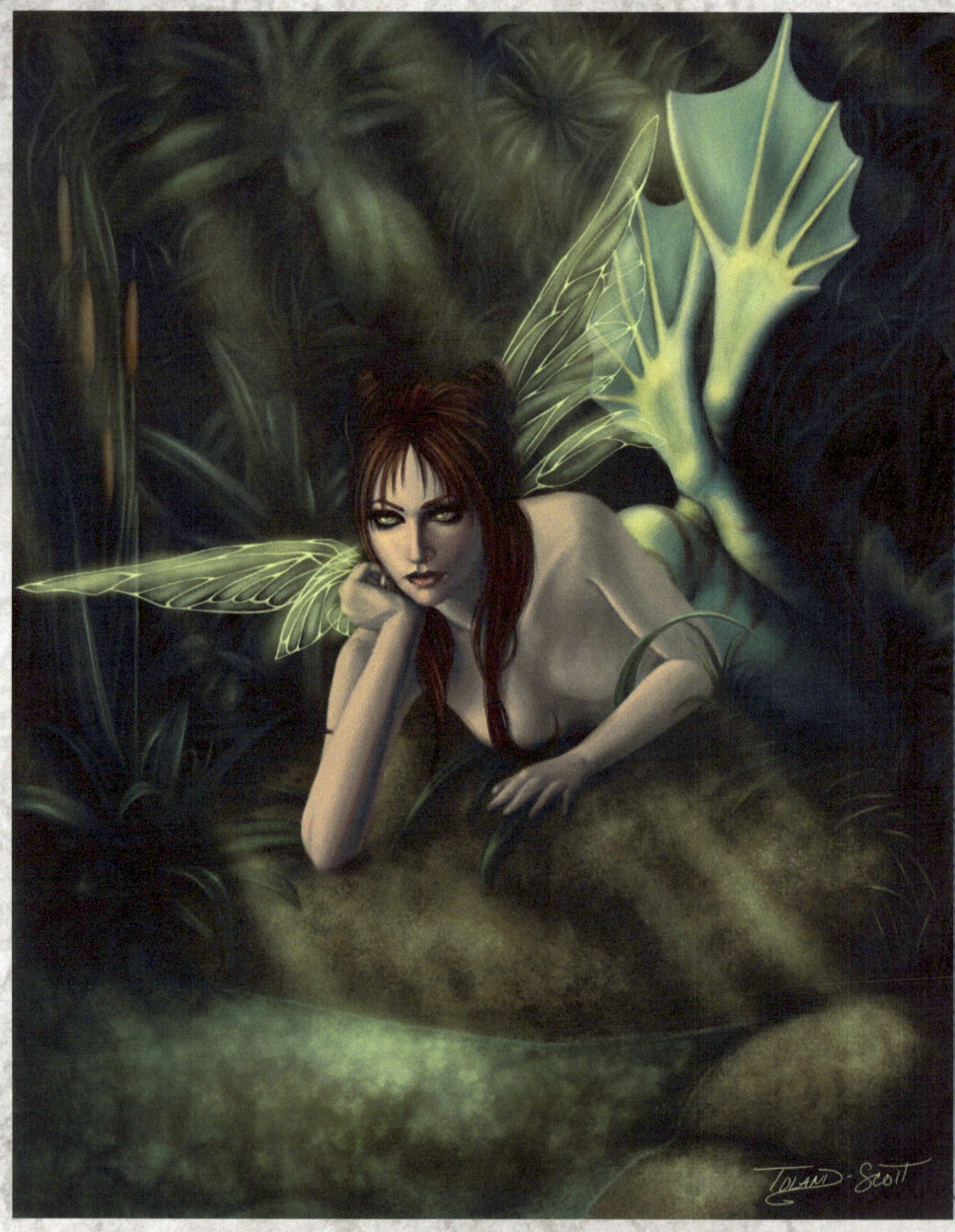

LATET ANGUIS IN HERBA - "Snake in the grass" is a continuation of my strange fascination with bizarre aquatic mythical creatures. This faerie-frog-mermaid rests on a rock, unaware of her surroundings or the snake lurking somewhere in the background.

This was painted digitally in 2013.

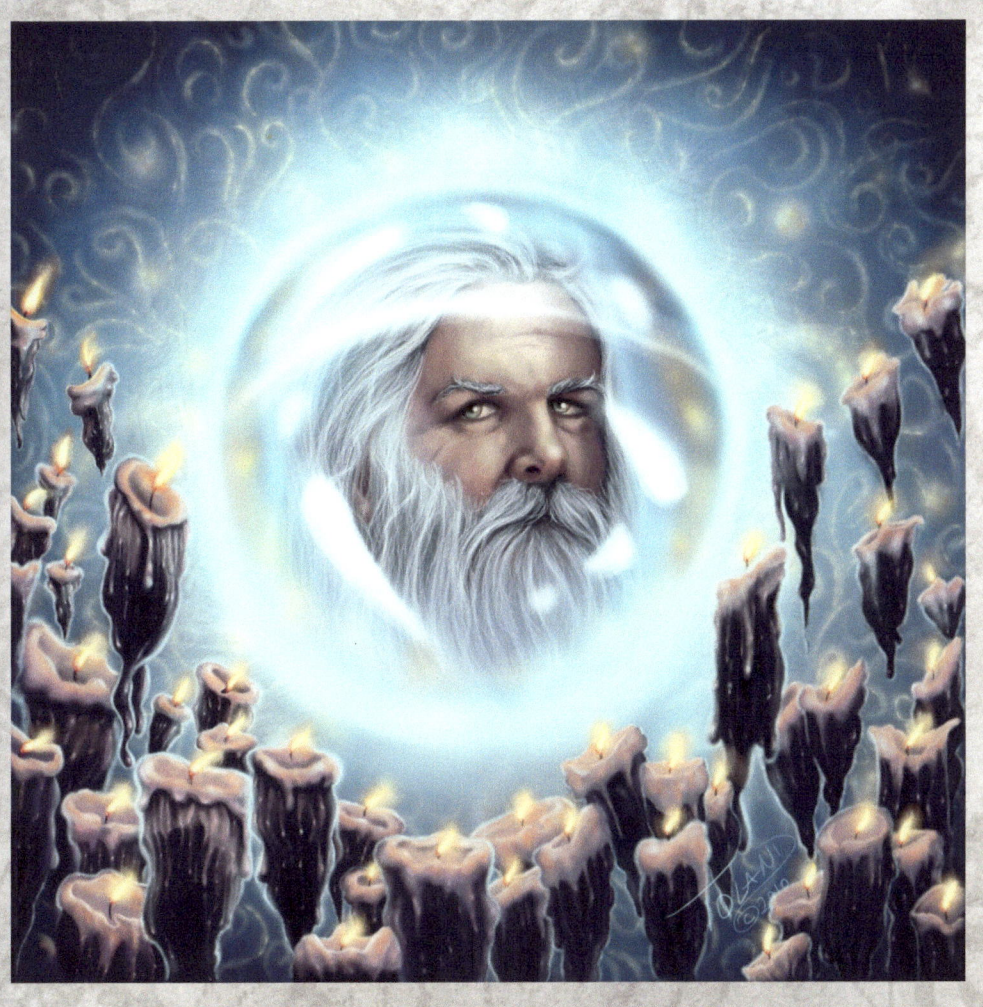

LOCKED WITHIN THE CRYSTAL BALL - The Hierophant is a card all about tradition, so it seemed a good idea to keep it traditional and represent this card with a man. Like the title states, this wizard has found himself trapped inside of his own crystal ball. Surrounded by floating candles, this card is steeped in magic.

This was painted digitally in 2010.

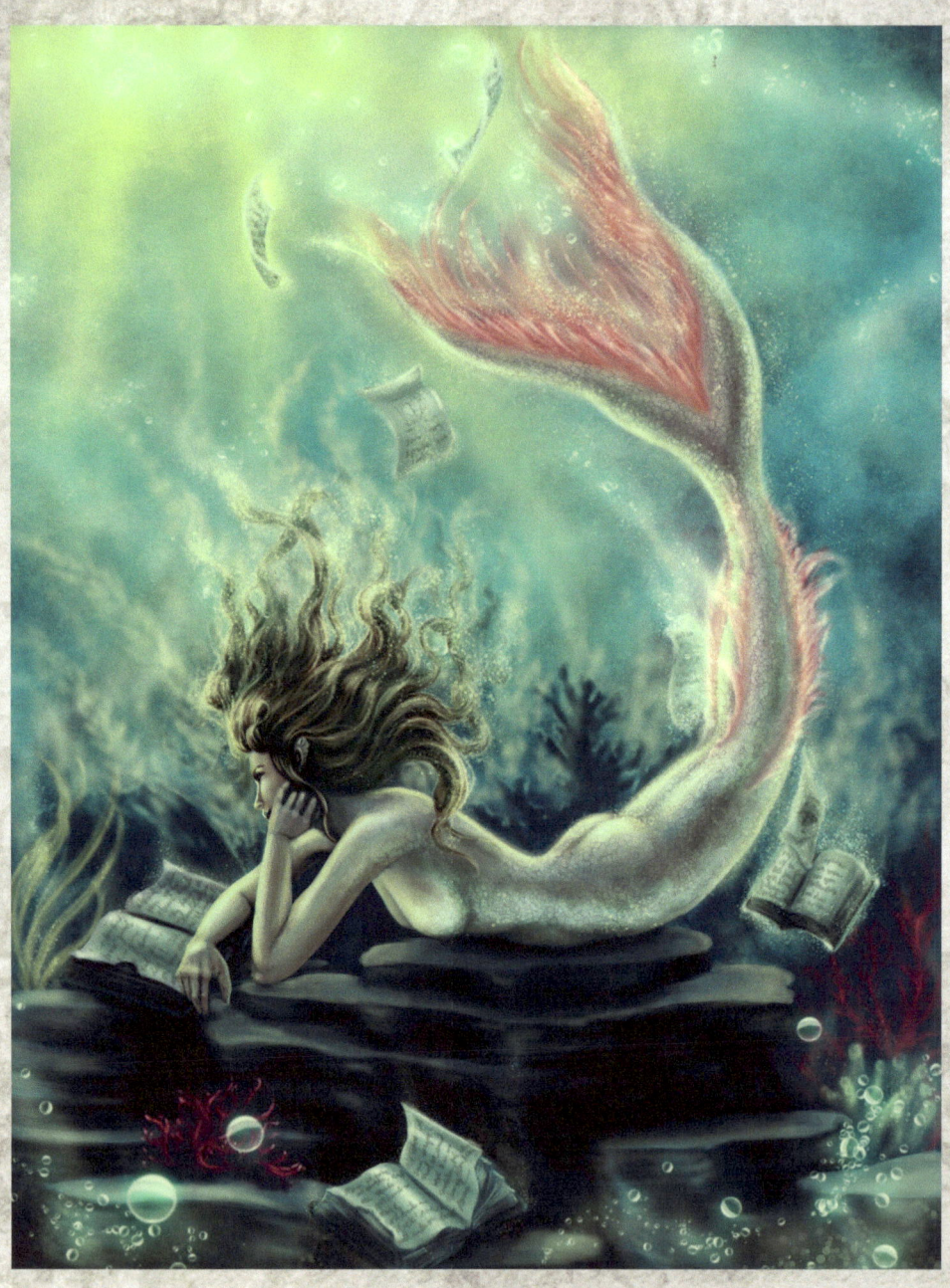

LOST BOOKS - I don't know where the weird images that pop into my mind come from, but this one was inspired by a Sketch Fest prompt of the same name. I'm sure the prompter never imagined books being lost at sea, but it seemed perfectly reasonable to me.

This was painted digitally in 2012.

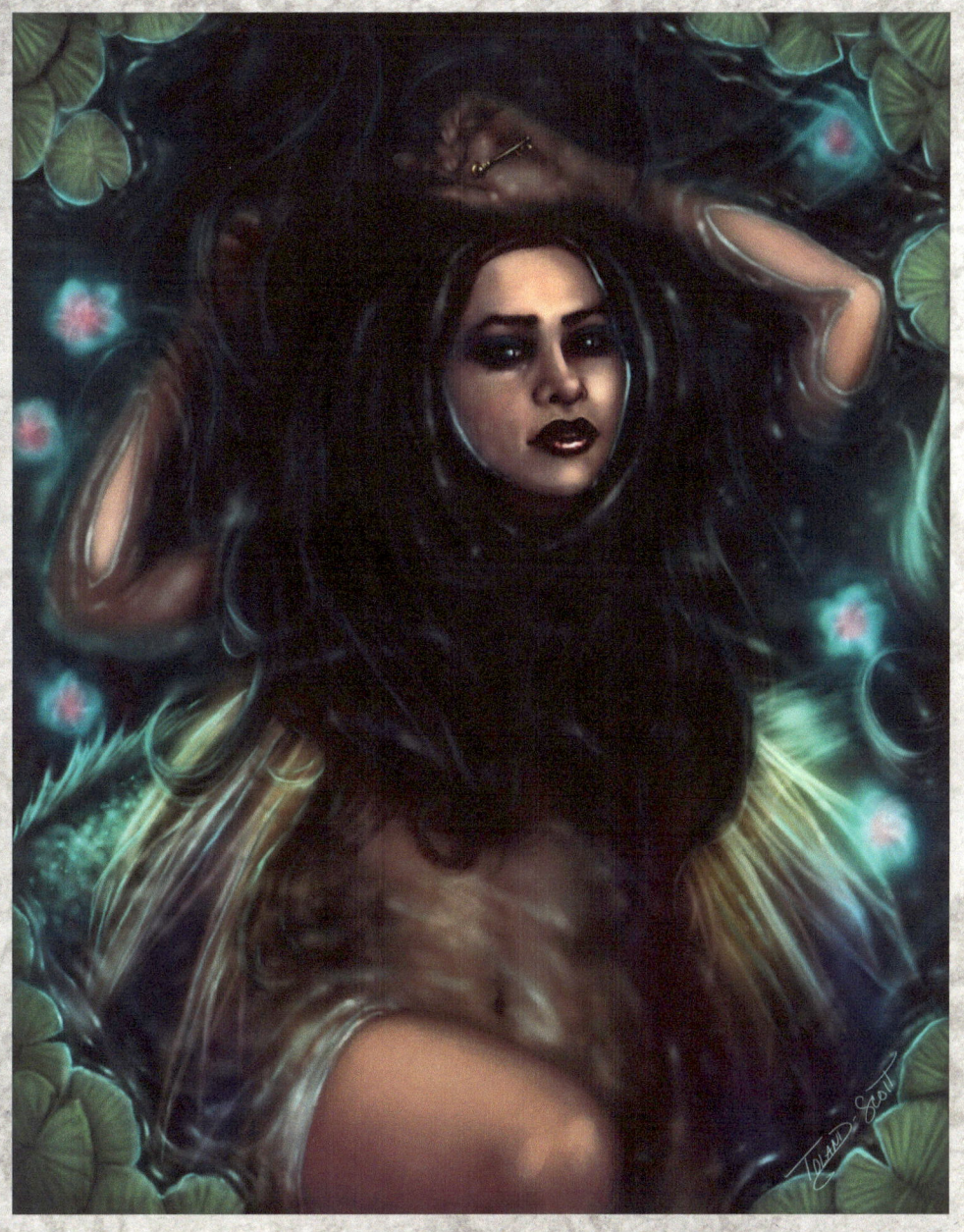

THE MARI-MORGANS - In Celtic mythology, Mari-Morgans are water-dwelling temptresses that trick young men into drowning themselves by showing them illusions of underwater castles and gardens. It probably doesn't hurt that these women are usually beautiful.

This was painted digitally in 2013.

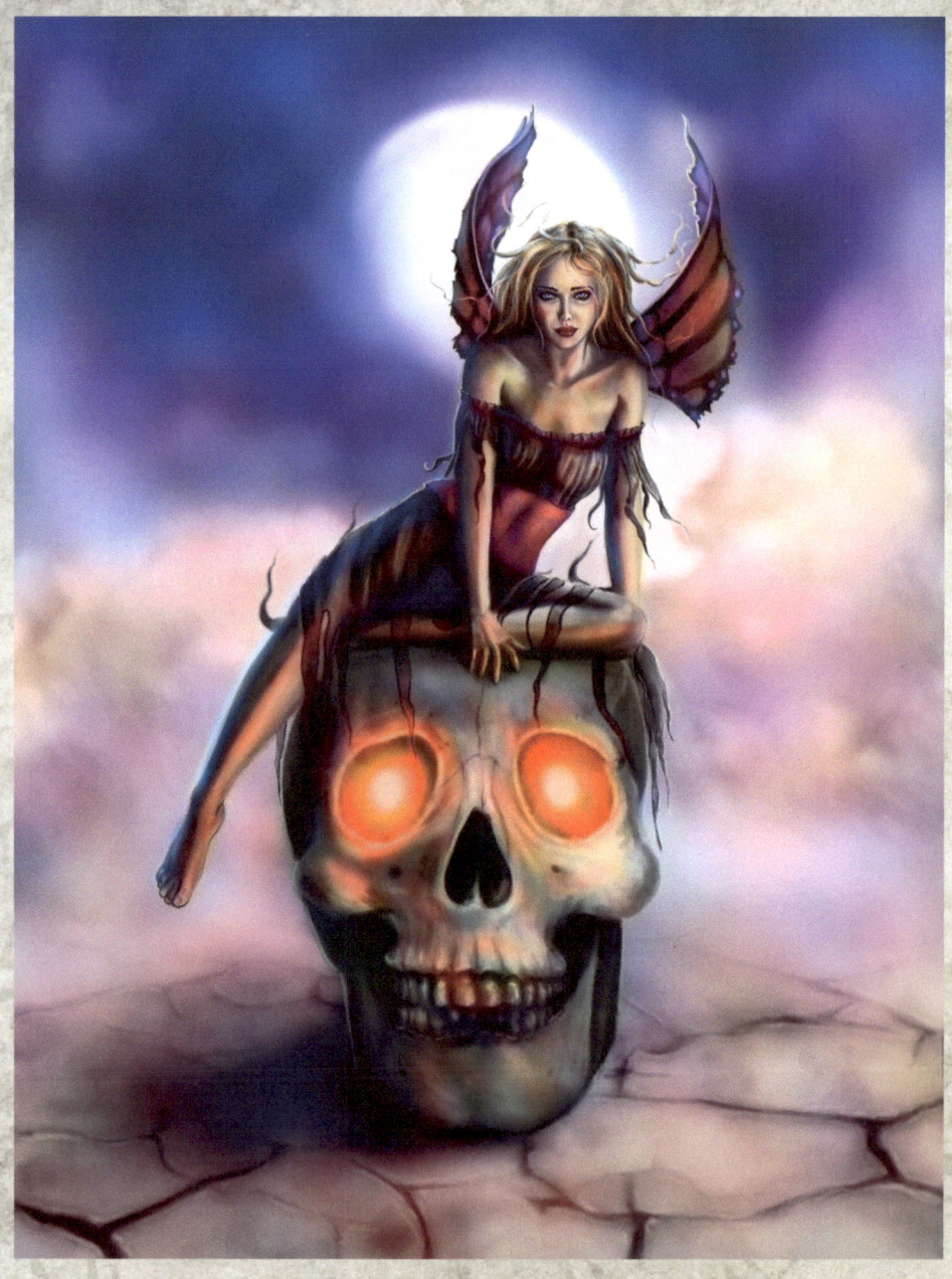

MEMENTO MORI - This faerie serves as a cute reminder that we are mortal and all things, including ourselves, must come to an end. Naturally, she represents Death in the oracle deck.

This was painted digitally in 2010.

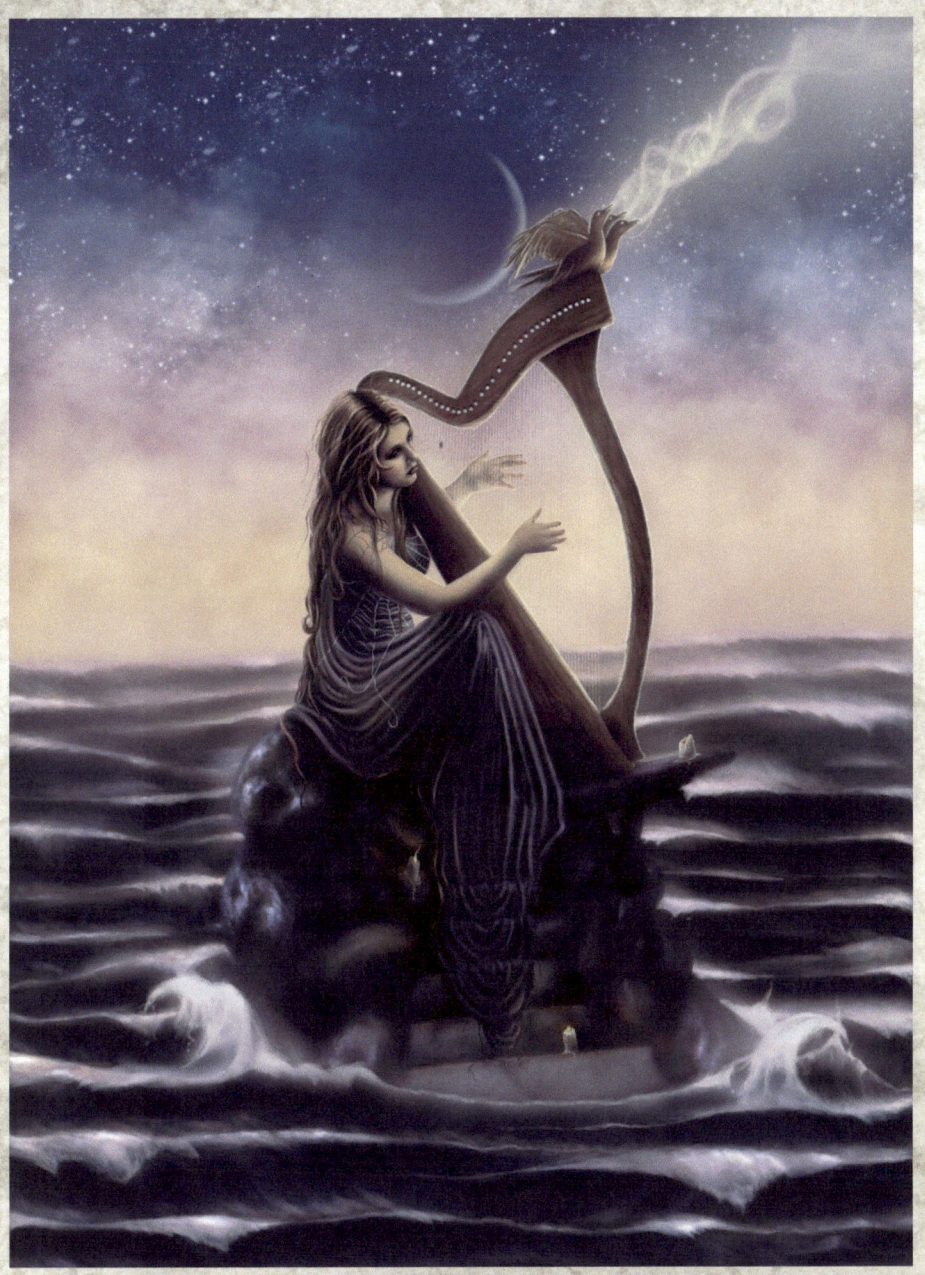

MOON'S SONG - A new day dawns over the ocean as this mysterious elf plays her enchanted harp. She brings the sun up, out of the ocean, and plays the moon to sleep. This card represents the New Dawn in the oracle deck.

This was painted digitally in 2009.

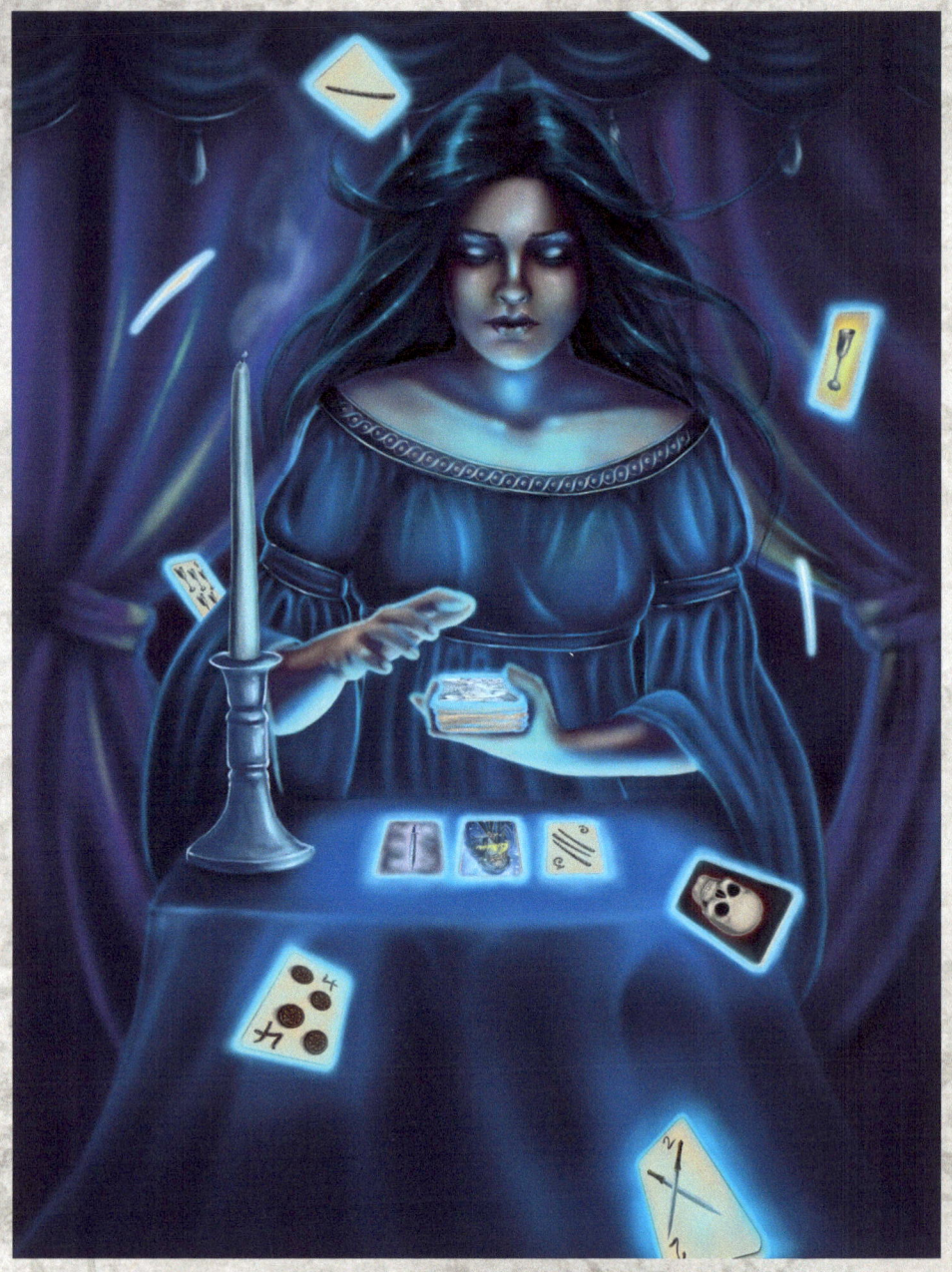

MIRRORS OF TIME - A fortune-teller painting in an oracle card deck? Why not! This card represents the Wheel of Fortune in the oracle deck.

This was painted digitally in 2009.

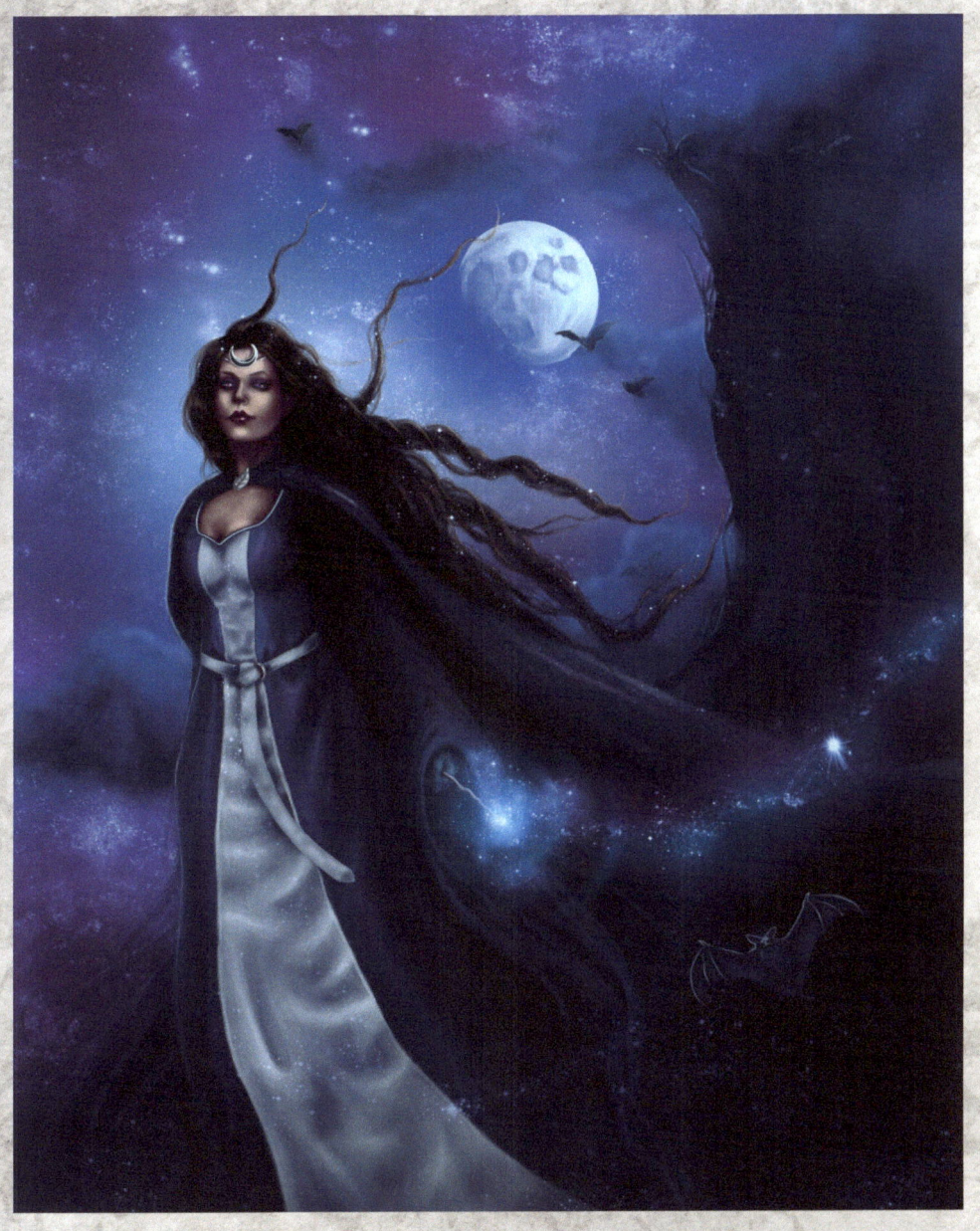

NYX - Goddess of the night sky, Nyx lends herself well to the Moon card in
the oracle deck. Mysterious and elusive, what lies in the darkness of her cloak is
uncertain and murky.

This was painted digitally in 2009.

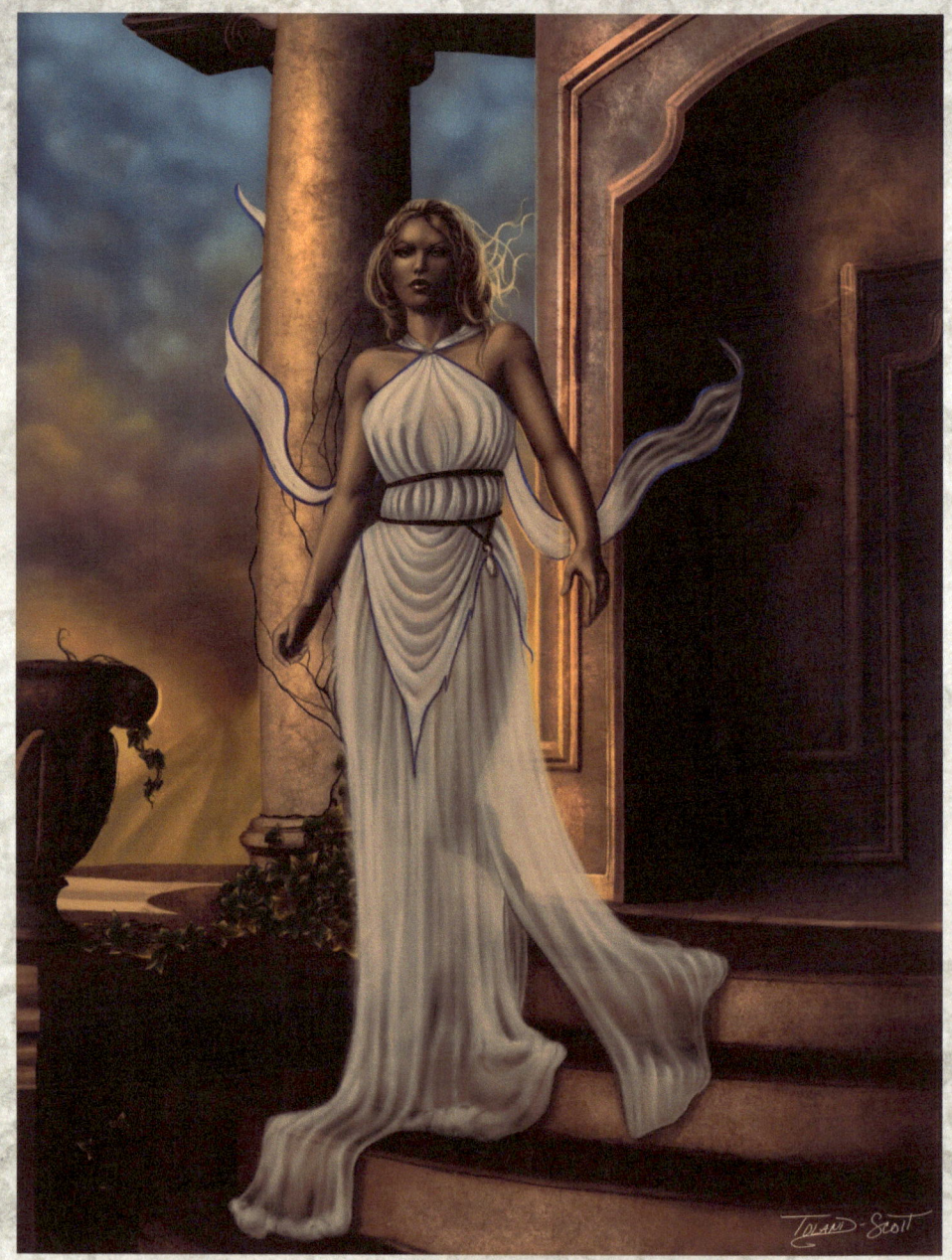

THE ORACLE OF POMPEII - Pompeii was a highly spiritual place just before the eruption of Mount Vesuvius. Temples were everywhere and for centuries after the famous eruption stories of oracles who foretold Pompeii's demise have been passed down through written and oral storytelling. This particular Oracle of Pompeii was inspired by the book, Last Days of Pompeii by Edward. G. Bulwer-Lytton.
This was painted digitally in 2013.

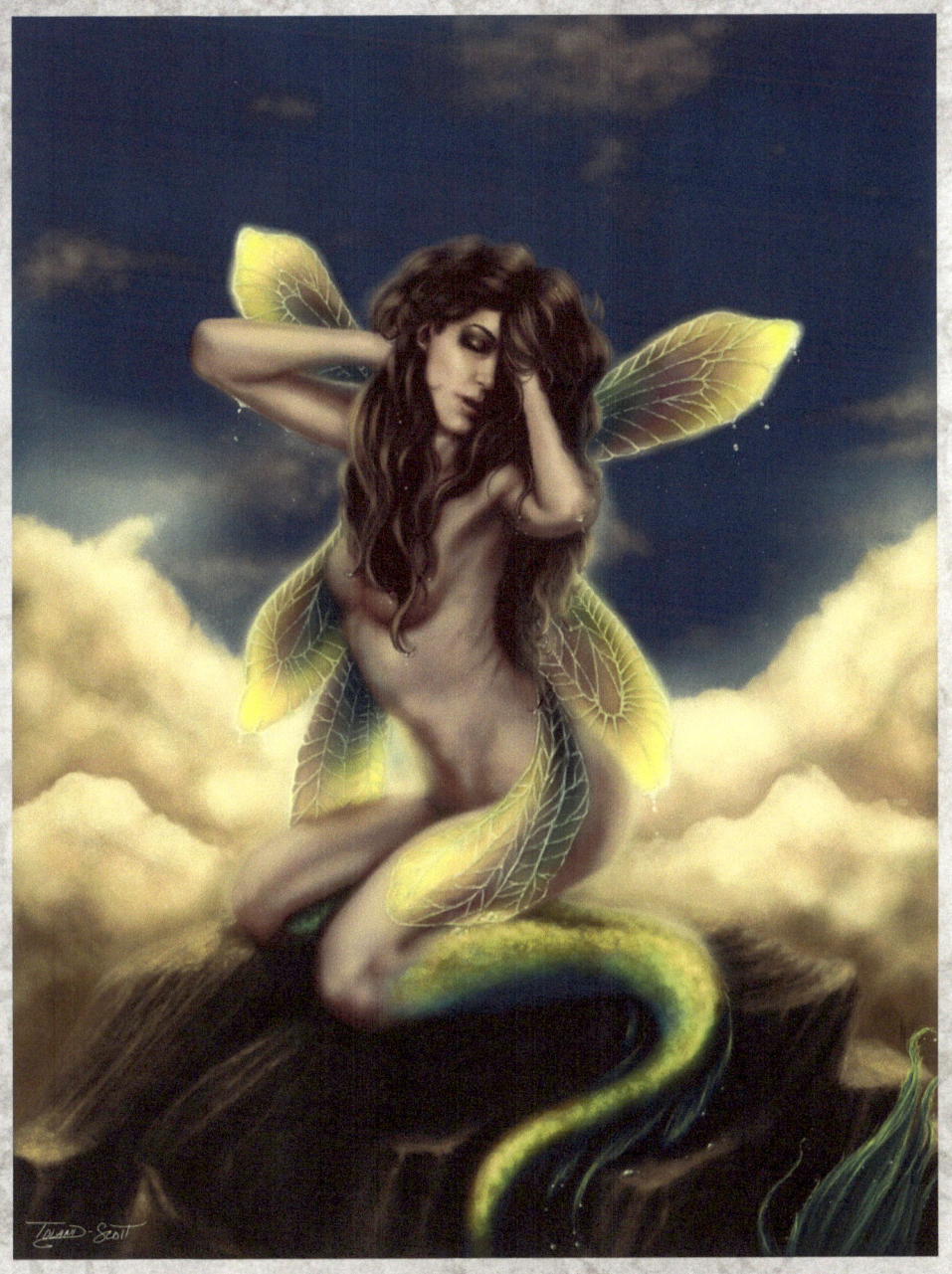

OUT TO DRY - Although mermaids are not typically associated with the air, there are countless mythological creatures that are essentially mermaids with wings. This mermaid represents Air in the oracle deck.

This was painted digitally in 2013.

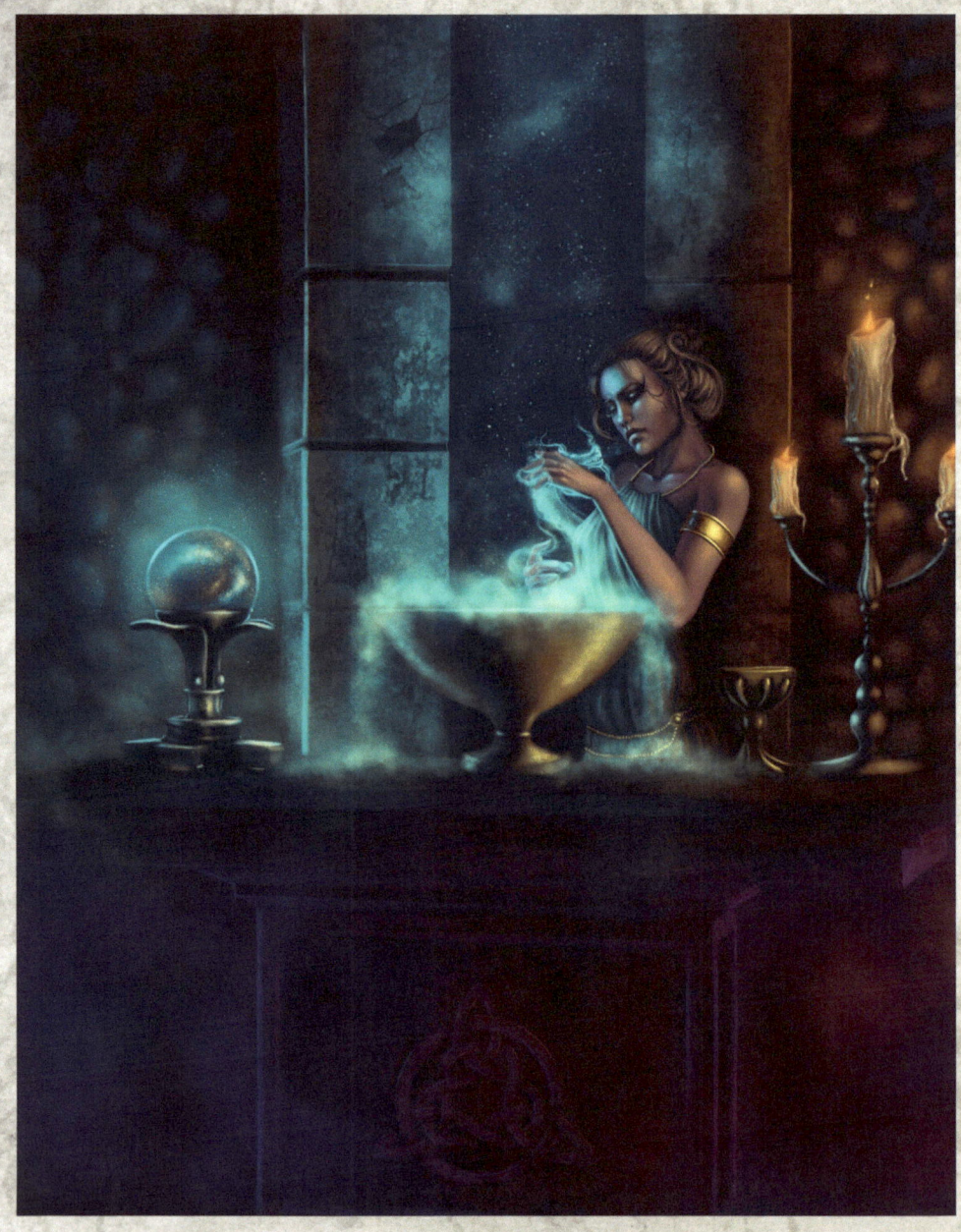

PHANTASMAL FAMILIAR - This witch is summoning a mystical dragon from her cauldron. I painted this image as a a Kickstarter reward, and although I cannot make any more prints of it, I can still include it in other things, like my oracle deck. This image represents Accomplishment.

This was painted digitally in 2012.

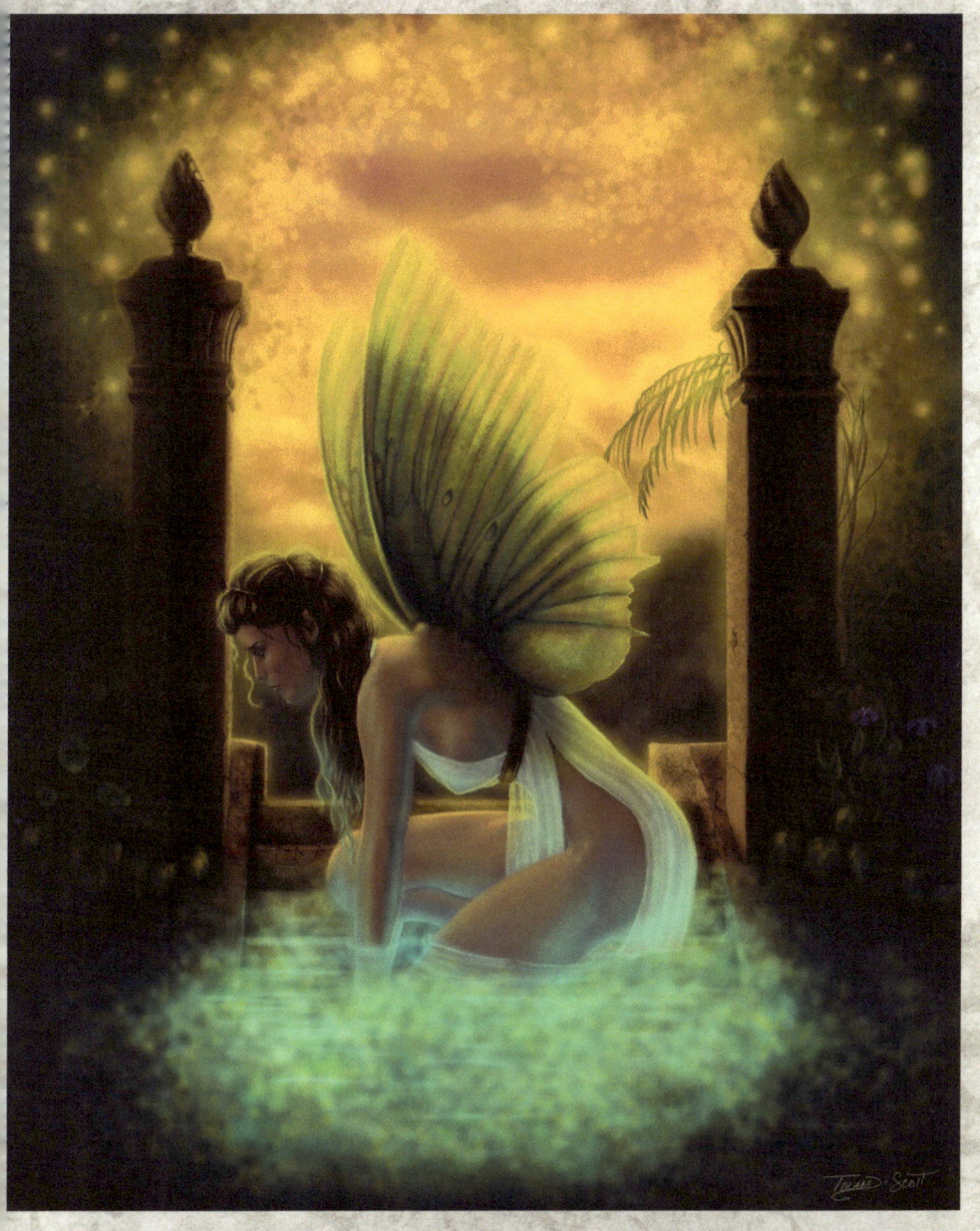

PORTAL TO ATLANTIS - Wouldn't it be great if there was a portal to the lost city of Atlantis? Visiting would be as simple as taking a dip in an enchanted pool. I frequently research similar lost cities for my mermaid paintings, and find the idea of Atlantis absolutely mesmerizing.

This was painted digitally in 2013.

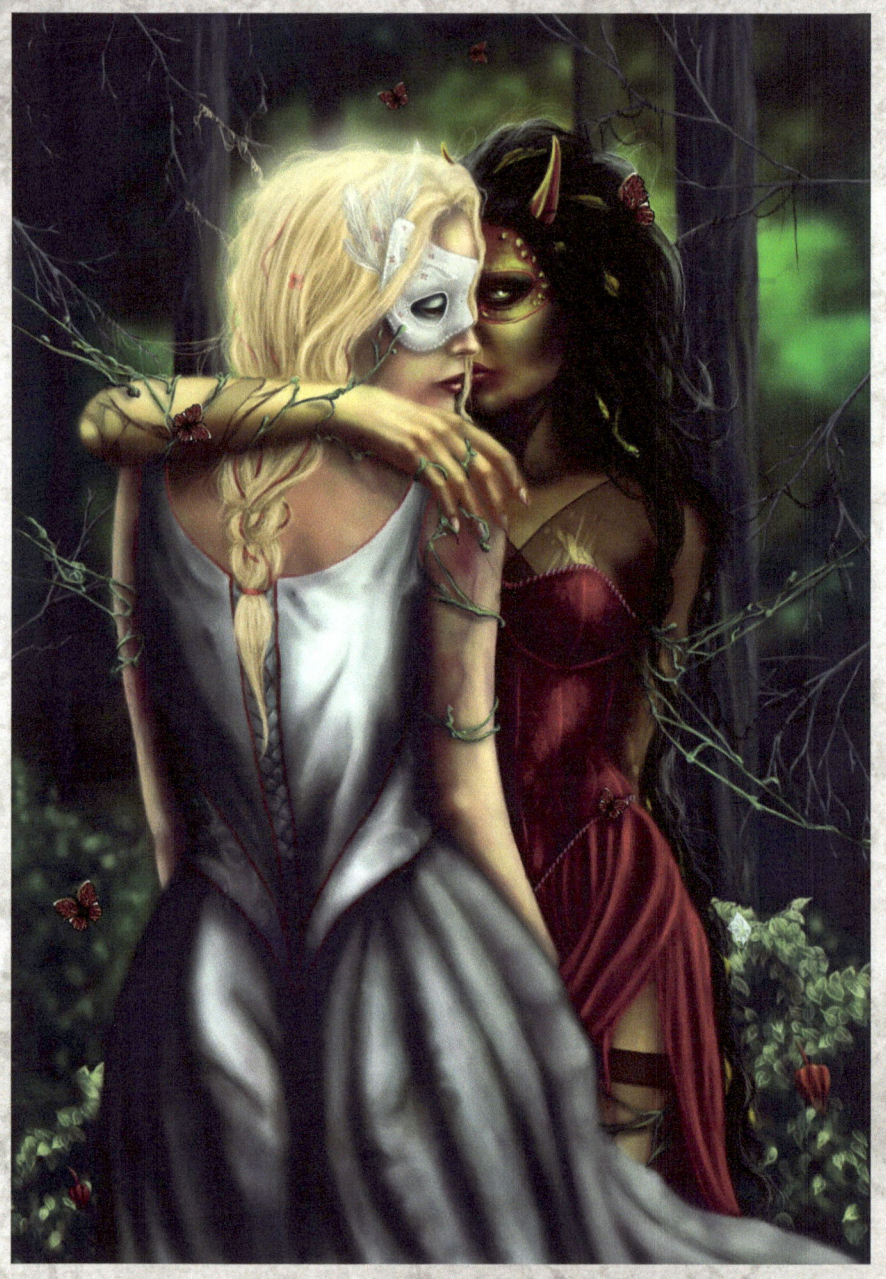

POSSESSED - This painting represents the two halves of all people. Light and dark live side by side inside each person, no matter which side they choose to show the world. This card represents The Lovers in the oracle deck, a card about duality.

This was painted digitally in 2009.

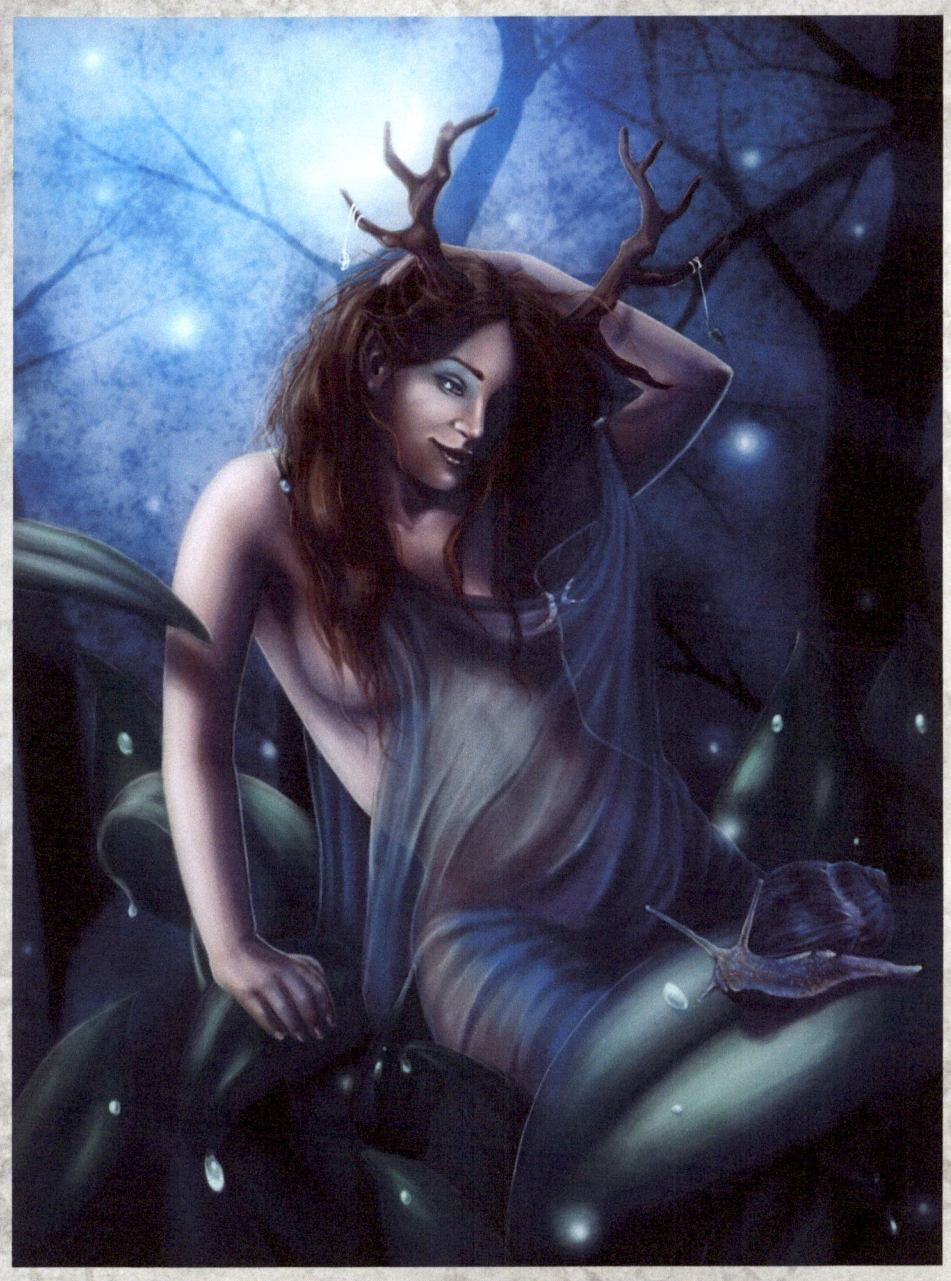

QUEEN OF THE WOOD - Here she is again, that horned goddess from the first page. In this case she represents things that are out of your control, Fate and Fortune.

This was painted digitally in 2009.

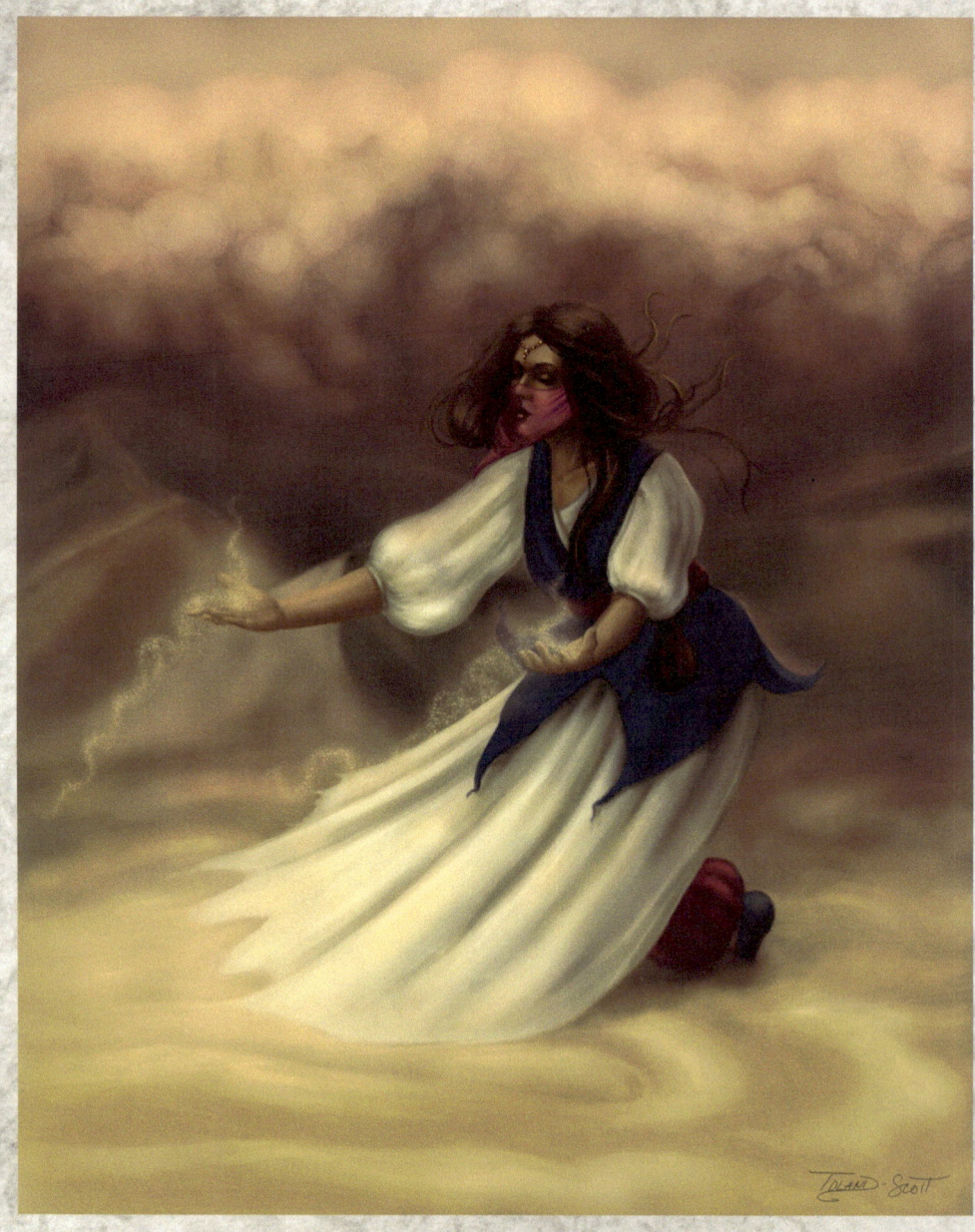

SAND WITCH - Another from a Sketch Fest prompt that I took in a weird direction. The prompt was actually for a drawing of a sandwich, but my imagination wasn't interested in that.

This was painted digitally in 2013.

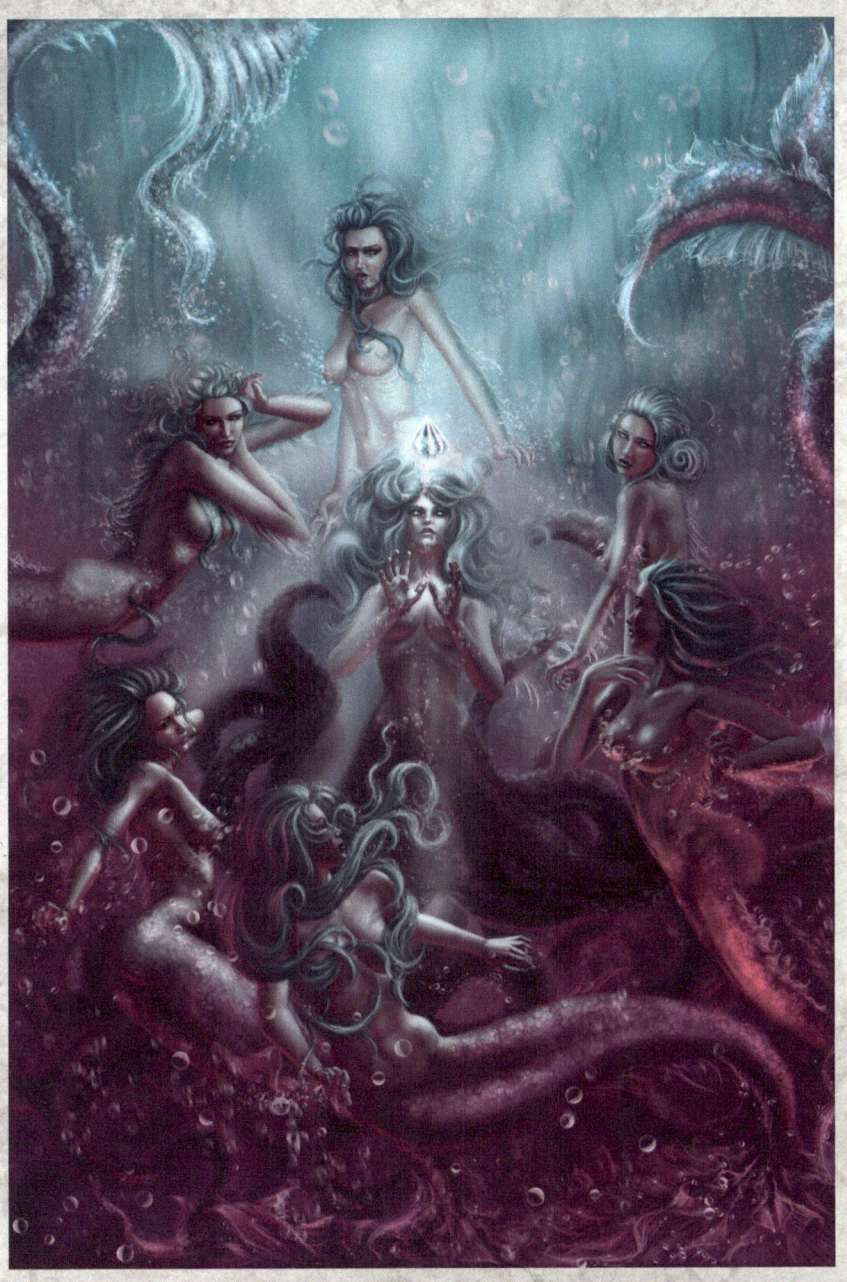

SEVEN SIRENS AND THE SILVER TEAR - The Queen of the Ocean is depicted here, surrounded by sirens, and giving up the ocean's greatest gifts to humanity. Some of the sirens seem unsure, while others are entranced.

This was painted digitally in 2012.

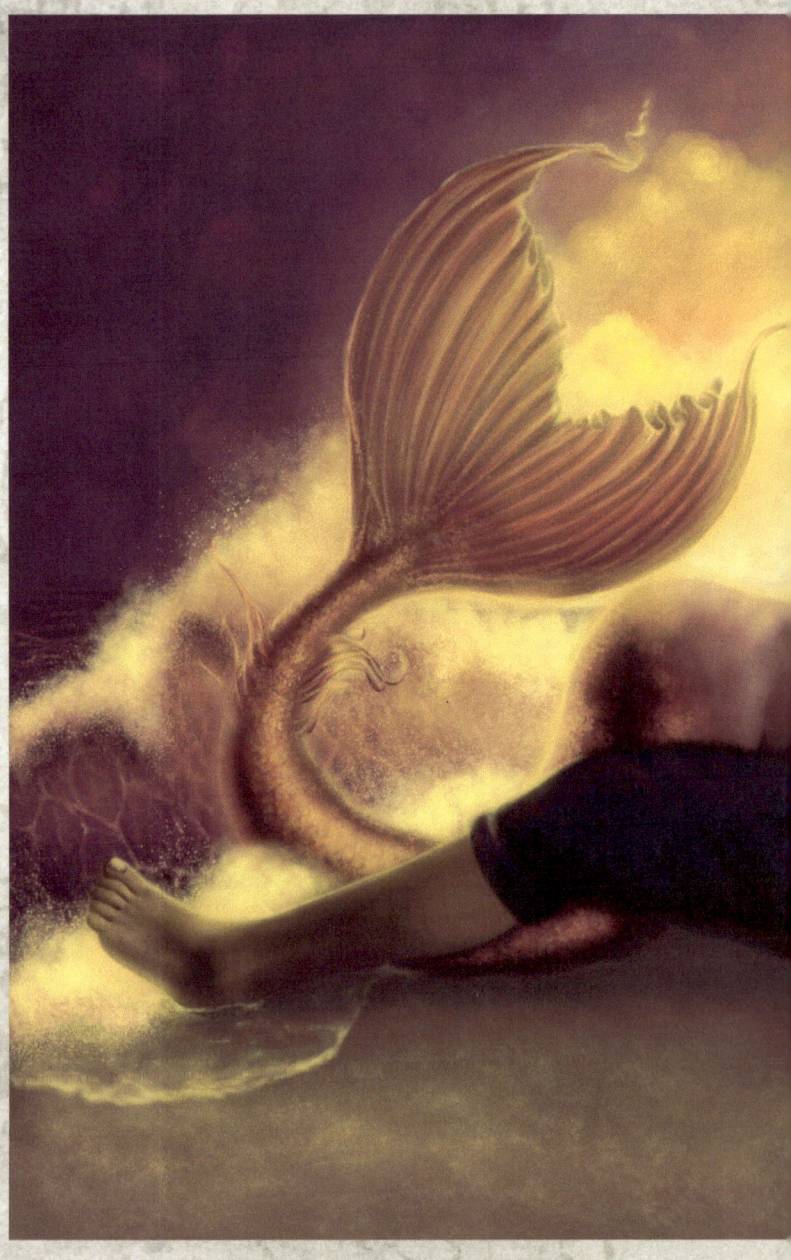

THE SIREN'S CATCH - Desperate to avoid being drowned by the siren, he
ties himself to the beach and hopes that it is enough to keep himself from running
into the water. Unfortunately for him, he can't remember why he is tied up
once he is under the siren's spell, and sees no problem with letting her cut him
loose with his own net knife.

This was painted digitally in 2013.

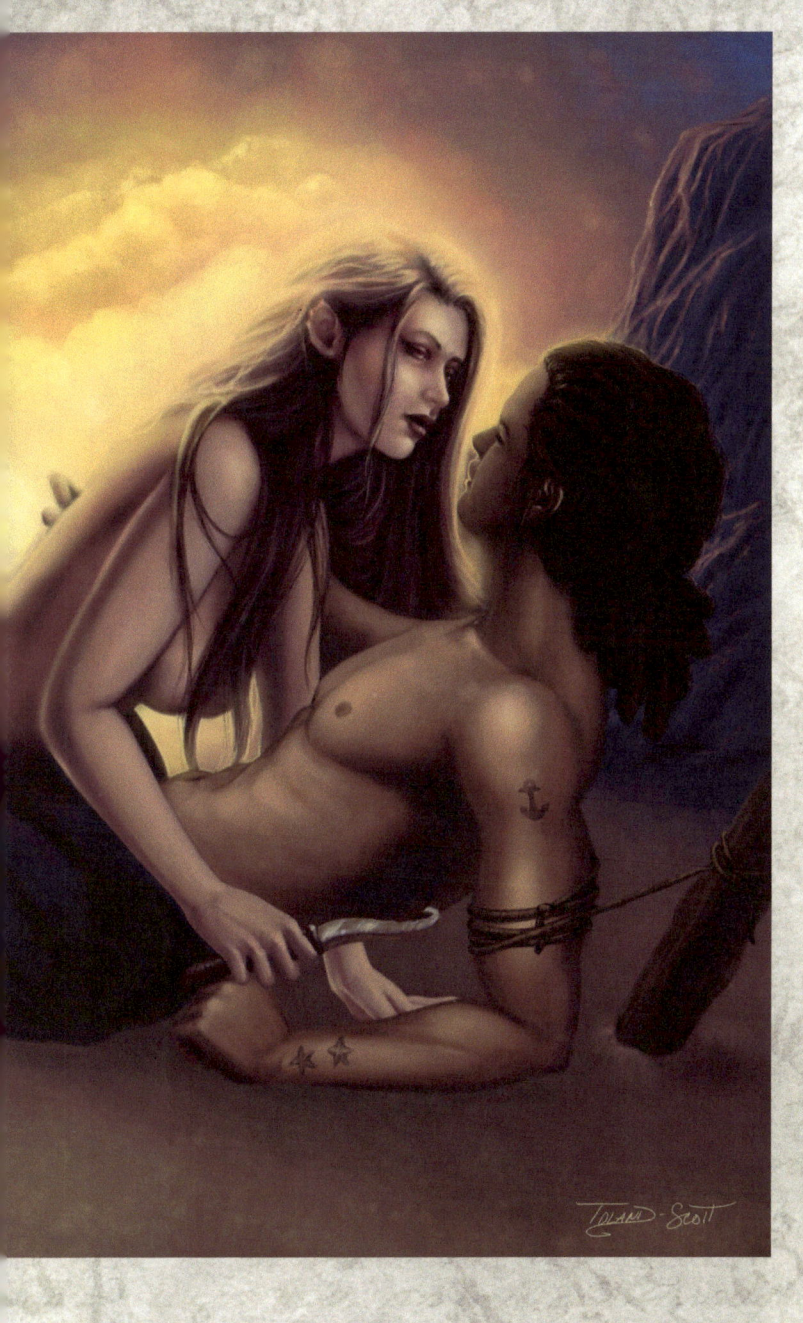

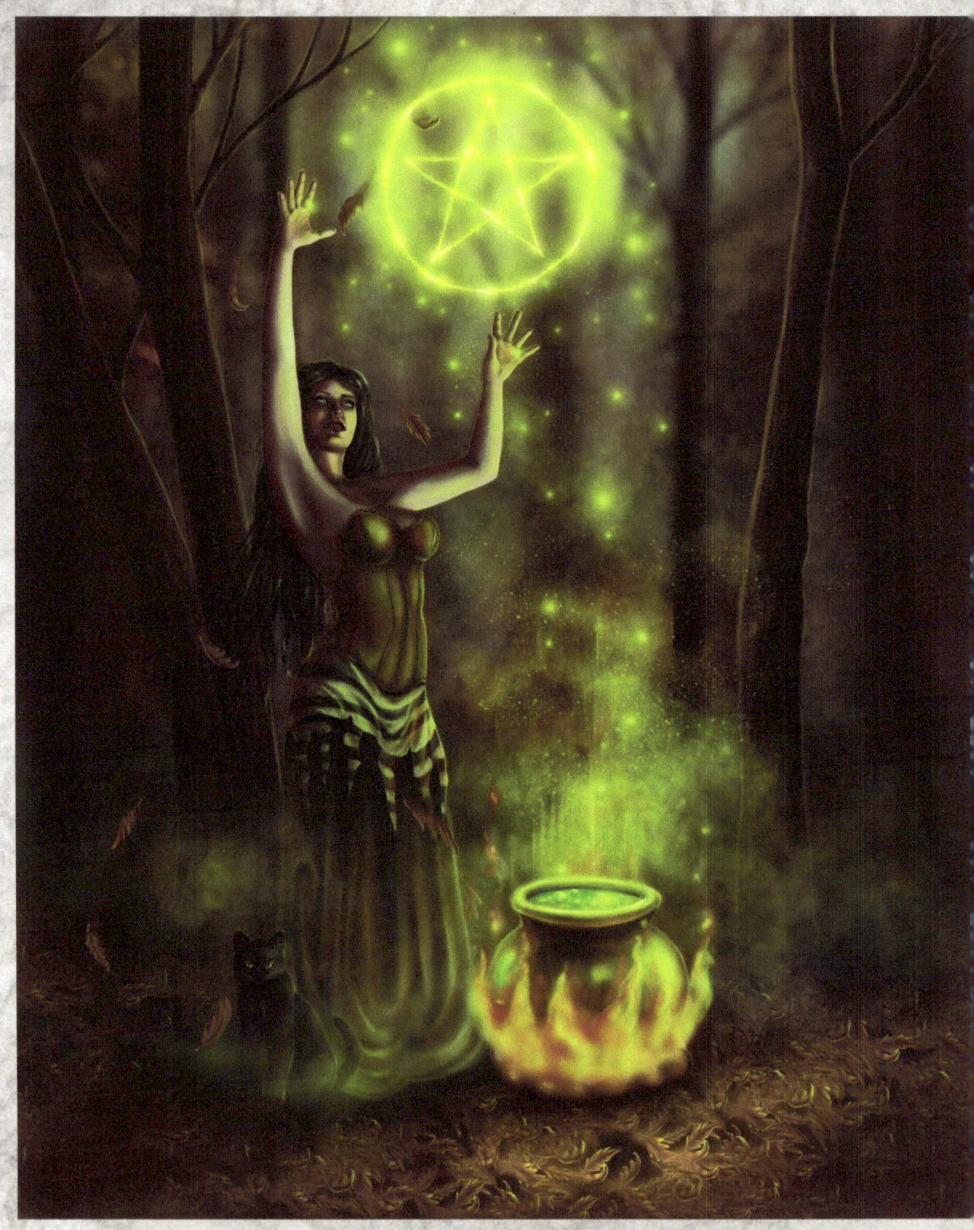

SPIRIT OF SAMHAIN - Samhain is the Gaelic festival that most Americans know now as Halloween. Samhain was believed to be the night when the veil between the living and the dead was the thinnest, and festivals of bonfires and feasts were held late into the night.

This was painted digitally in 2009.

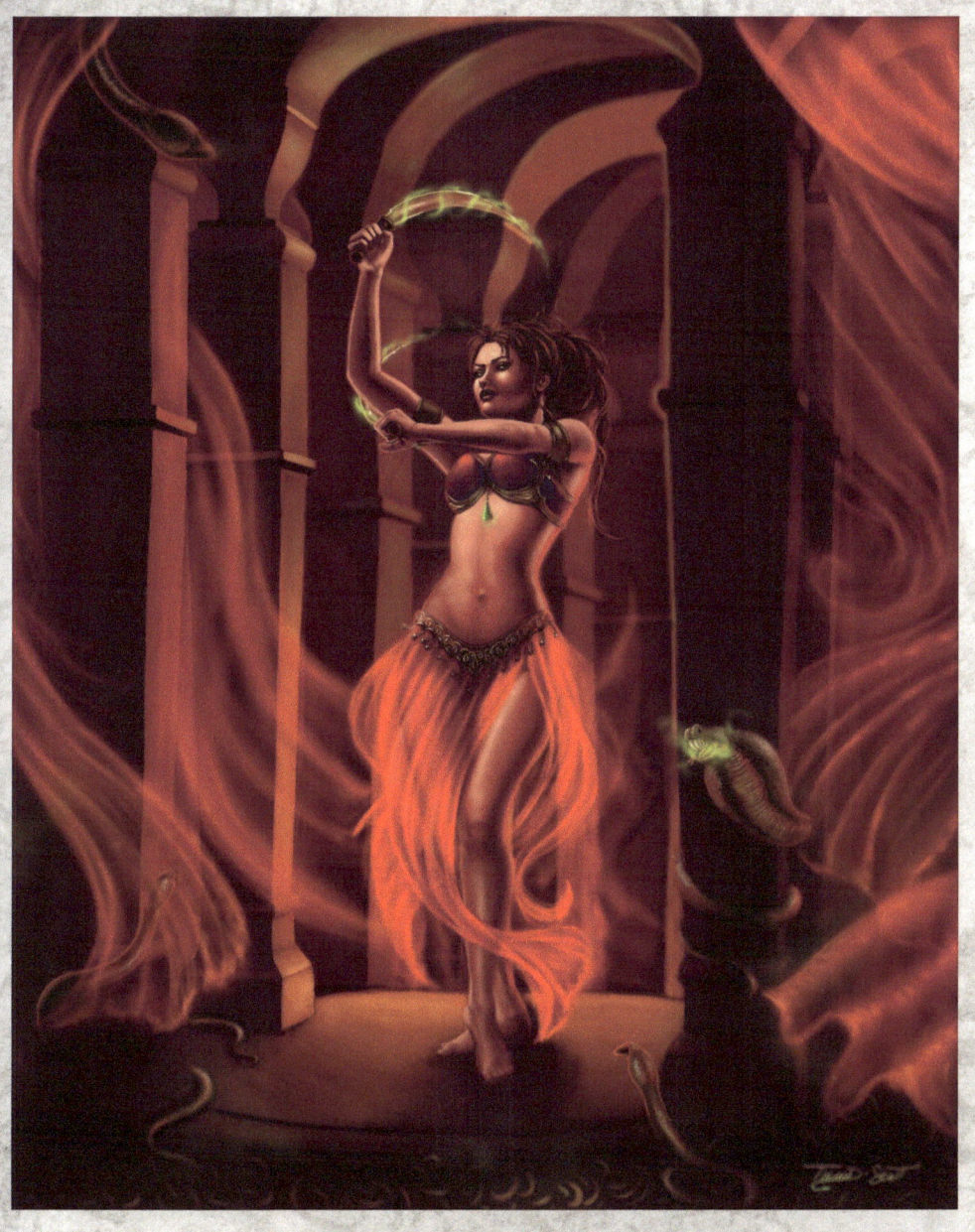

VENOM - This belly dancer continues with her dance despite the hundreds of deadly snakes surrounding her. Perhaps she's used to them, her knives seem to be emitting a venomous glow. She represents Strength in the oracle deck.

This was painted digitally in 2012.

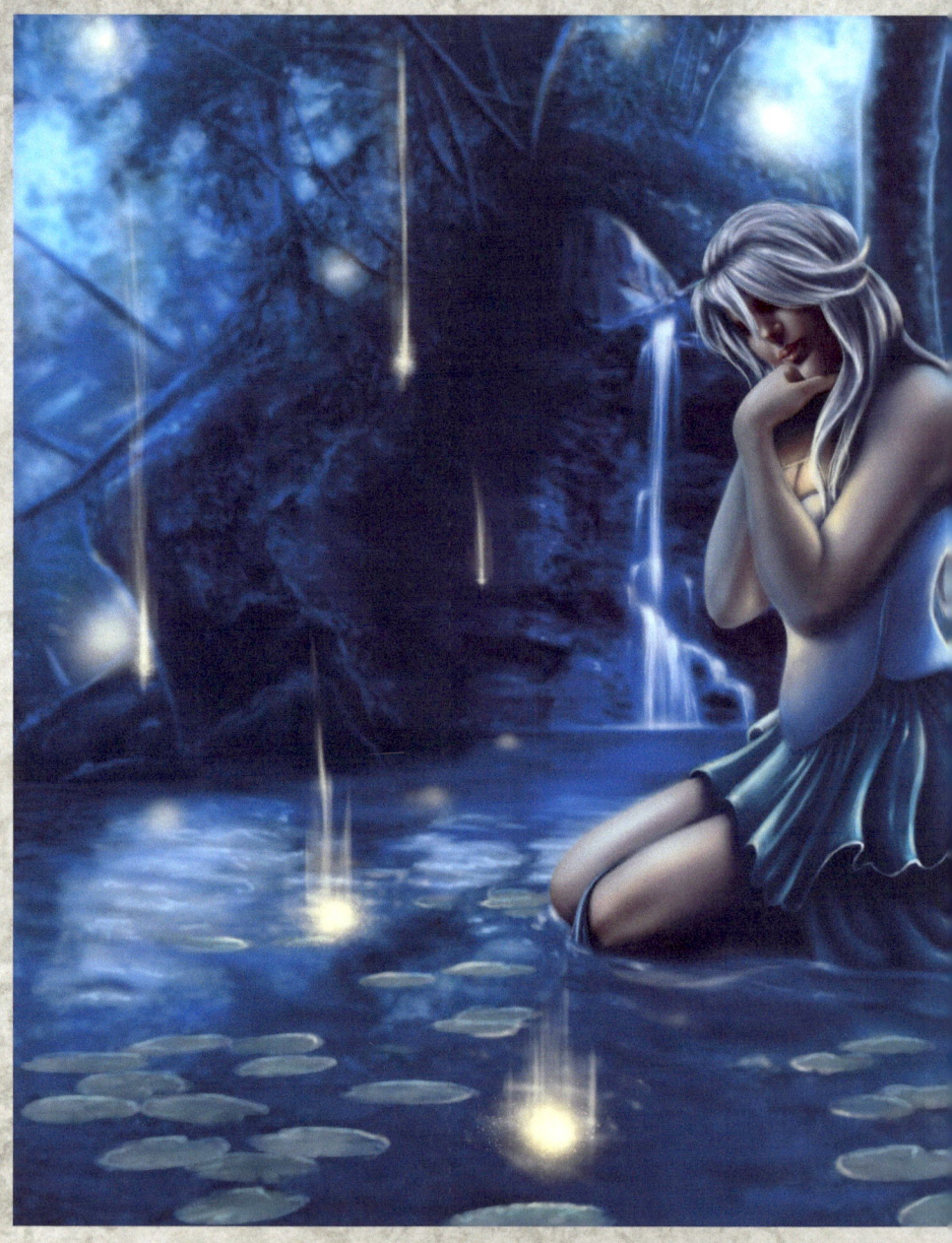

STARDUST - Representing The Star, this sweet faerie is a symbol of positive changes on the horizon. She is surrounded by falling stars and seems to have caught one for herself.

This was painted digitally in 2011.

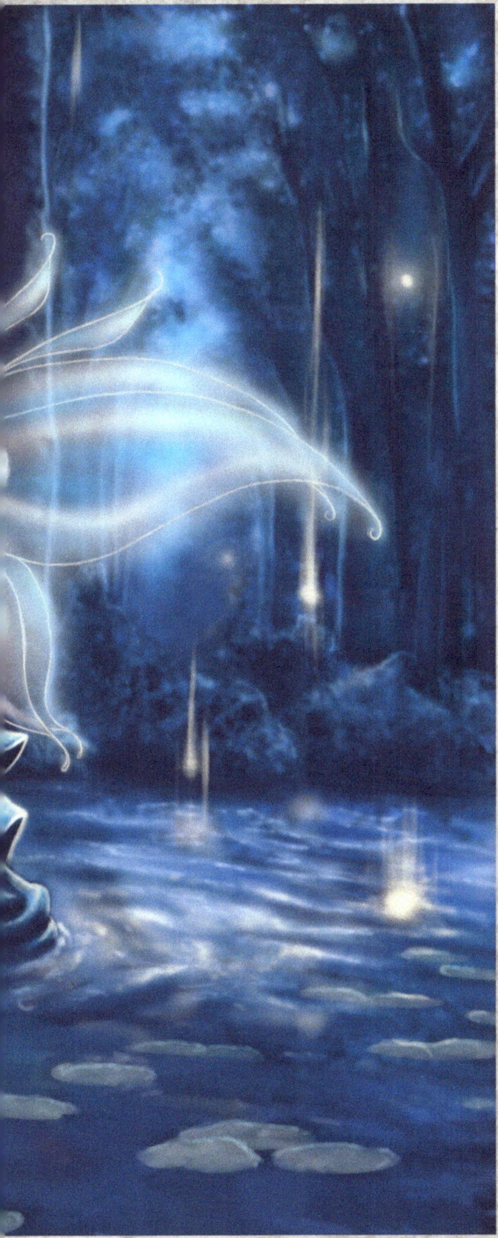

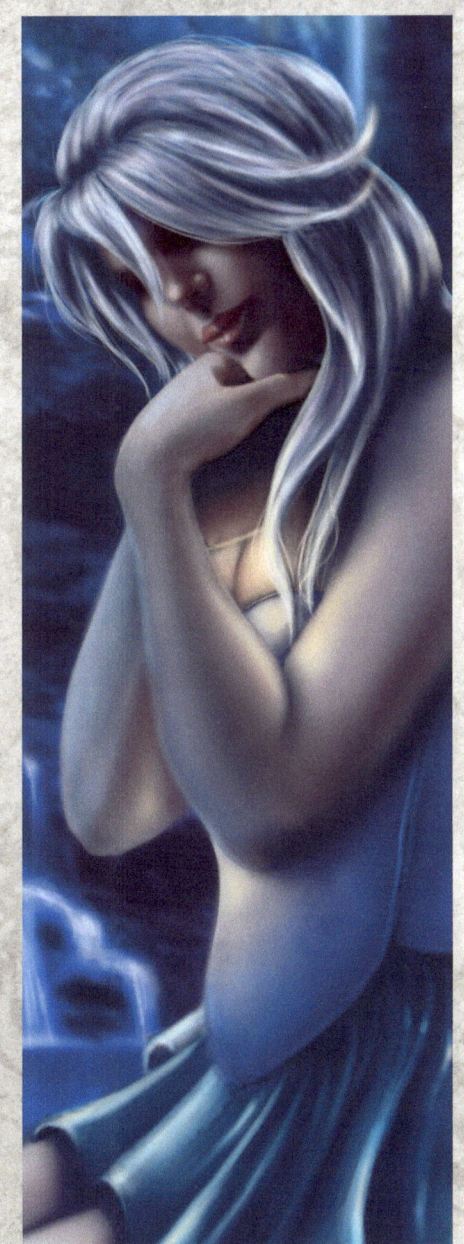

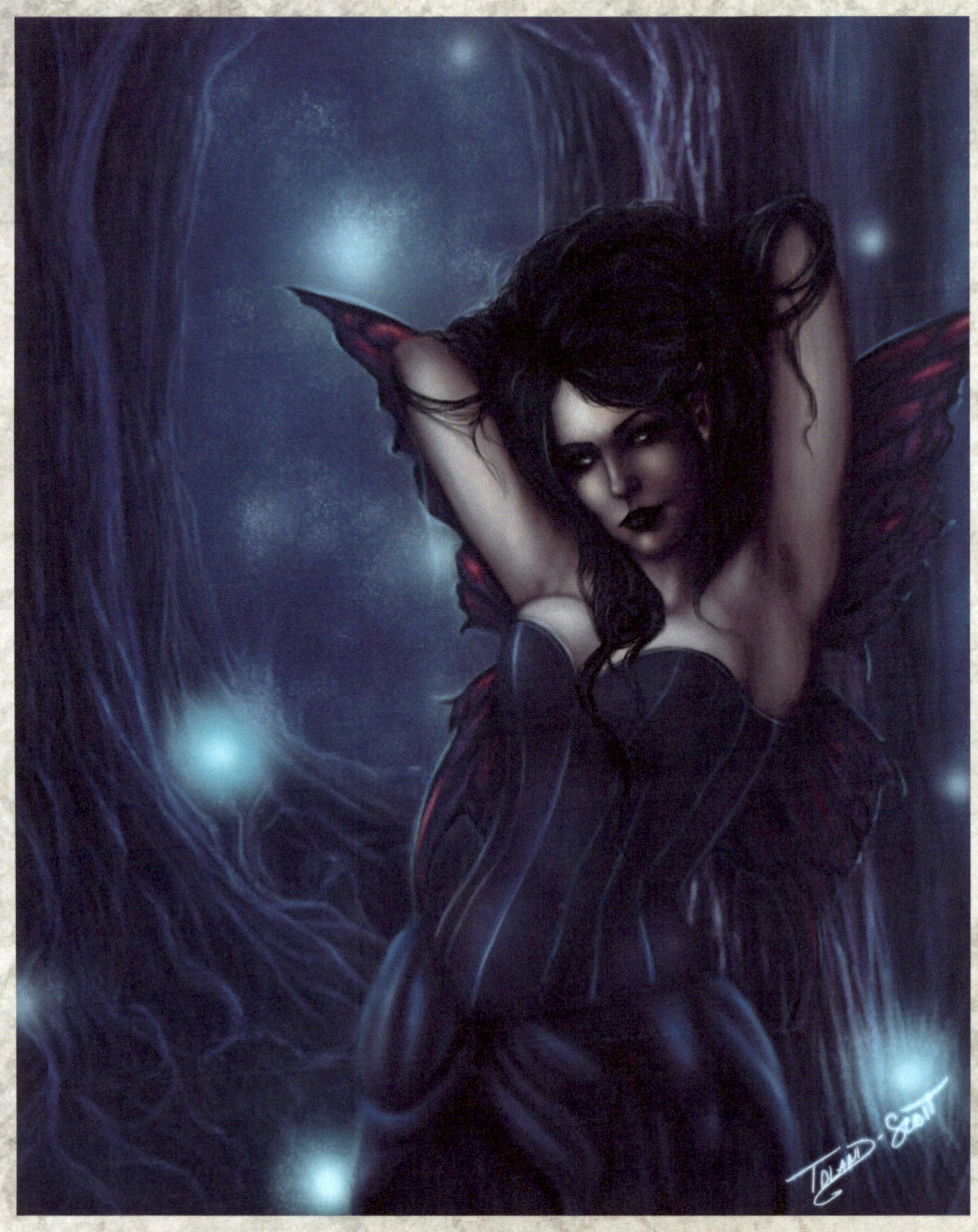

THE WILL-O-THE-WISP - Before people had a scientific understanding of the world, will-o-the-wisps were said to be faeries who lured people to their deaths near bogs, swamps, and bodies of water with strange ethereal lights. This painting represents The Devil, or Trickery, in the oracle deck.

This was painted digitally in 2012.

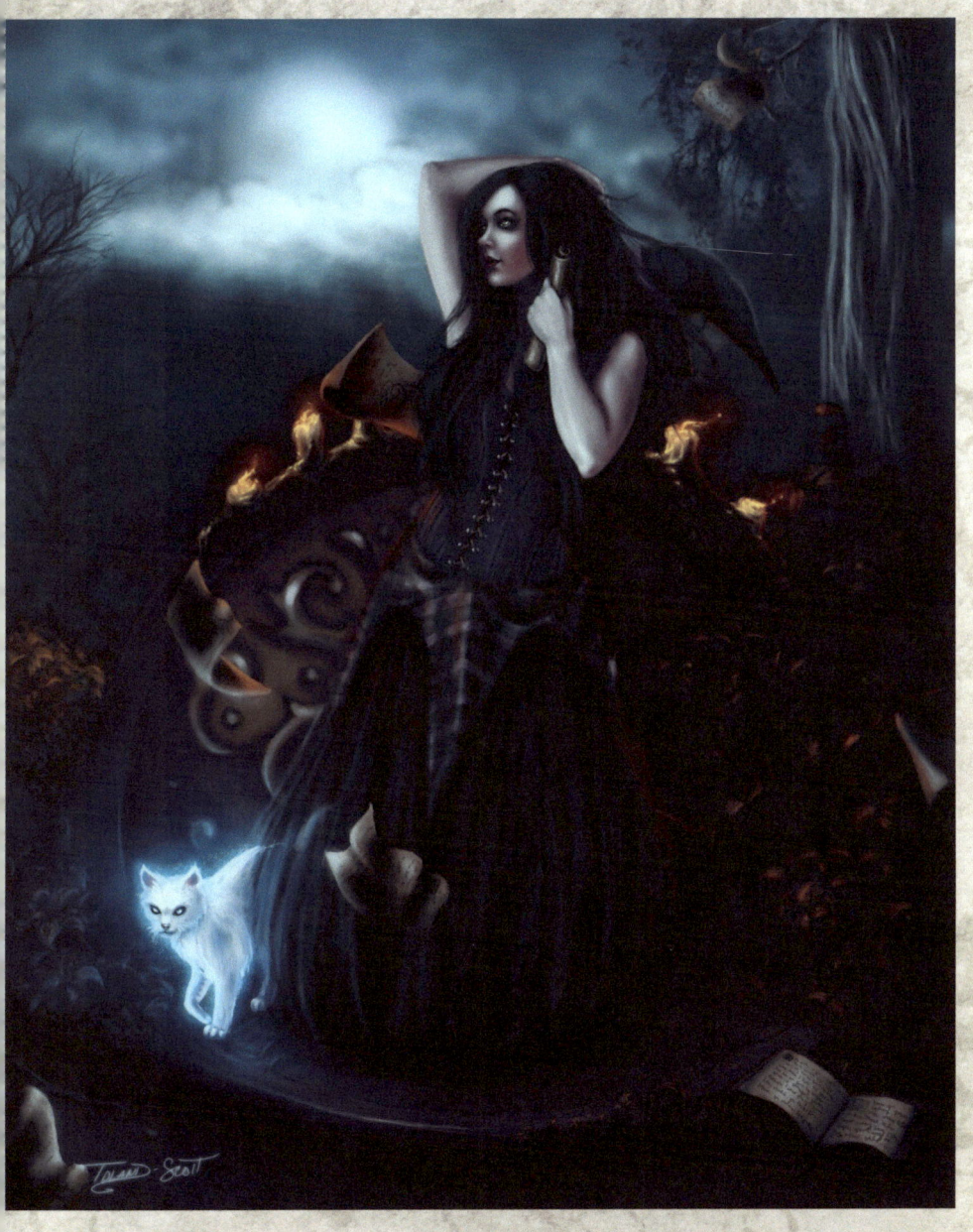

THE WITCHING HOUR - I painted this in memory of my beloved cat, Kerwin. He passed away shortly before Halloween, and just a few days later two stray cats, a mother and her kitten, showed up on my doorstep. They've lived with us ever since.

This was painted digitally in 2012.

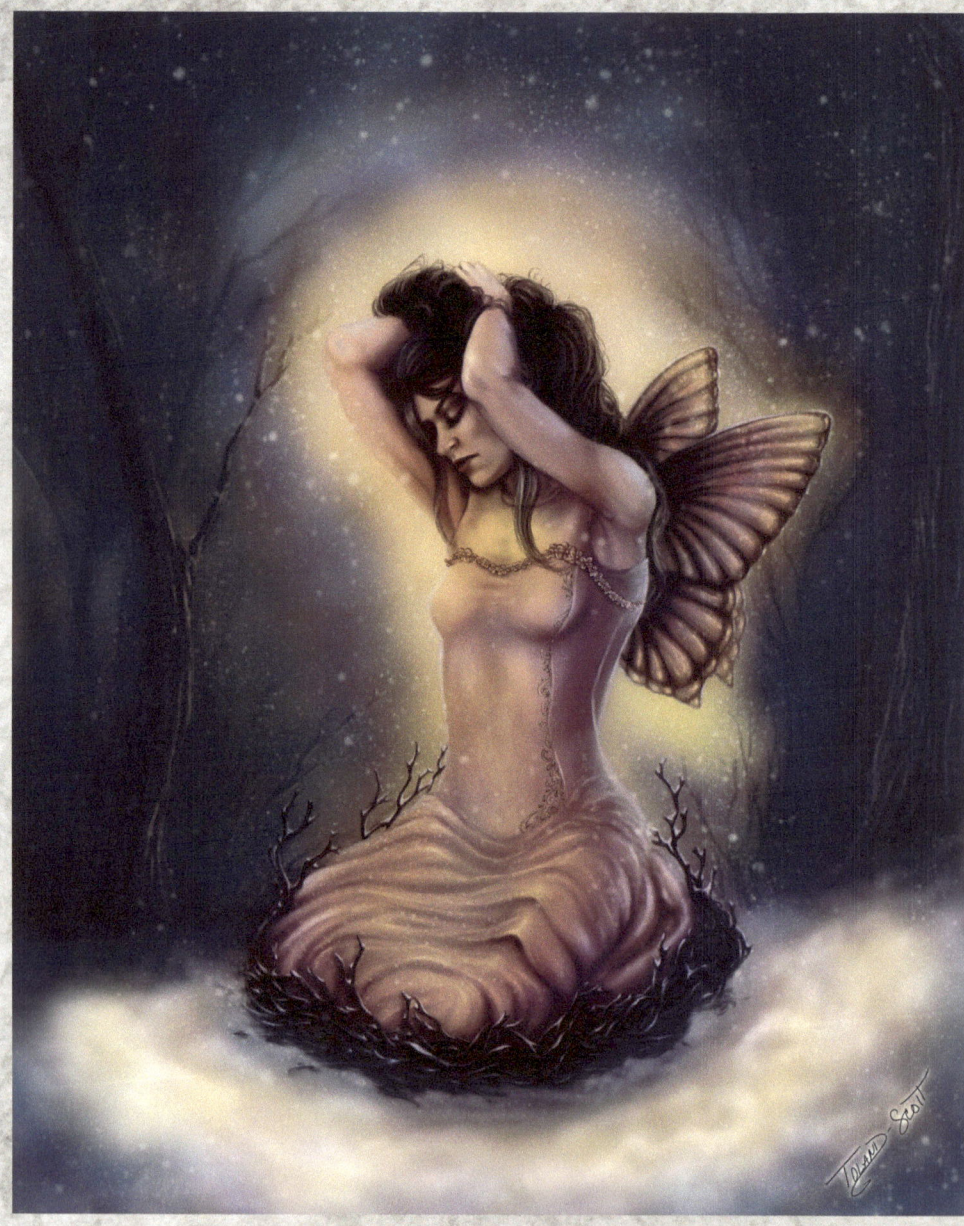

WINTERBORN - I sketched the figure of this faerie but I wasn't sure what I wanted to do with it. Suddenly the image of a sweet faerie awakening in a giant bird's nest popped into my mind, and I knew she was perfect for it. She represents Growth in the oracle deck.

This was painted digitally in 2012.

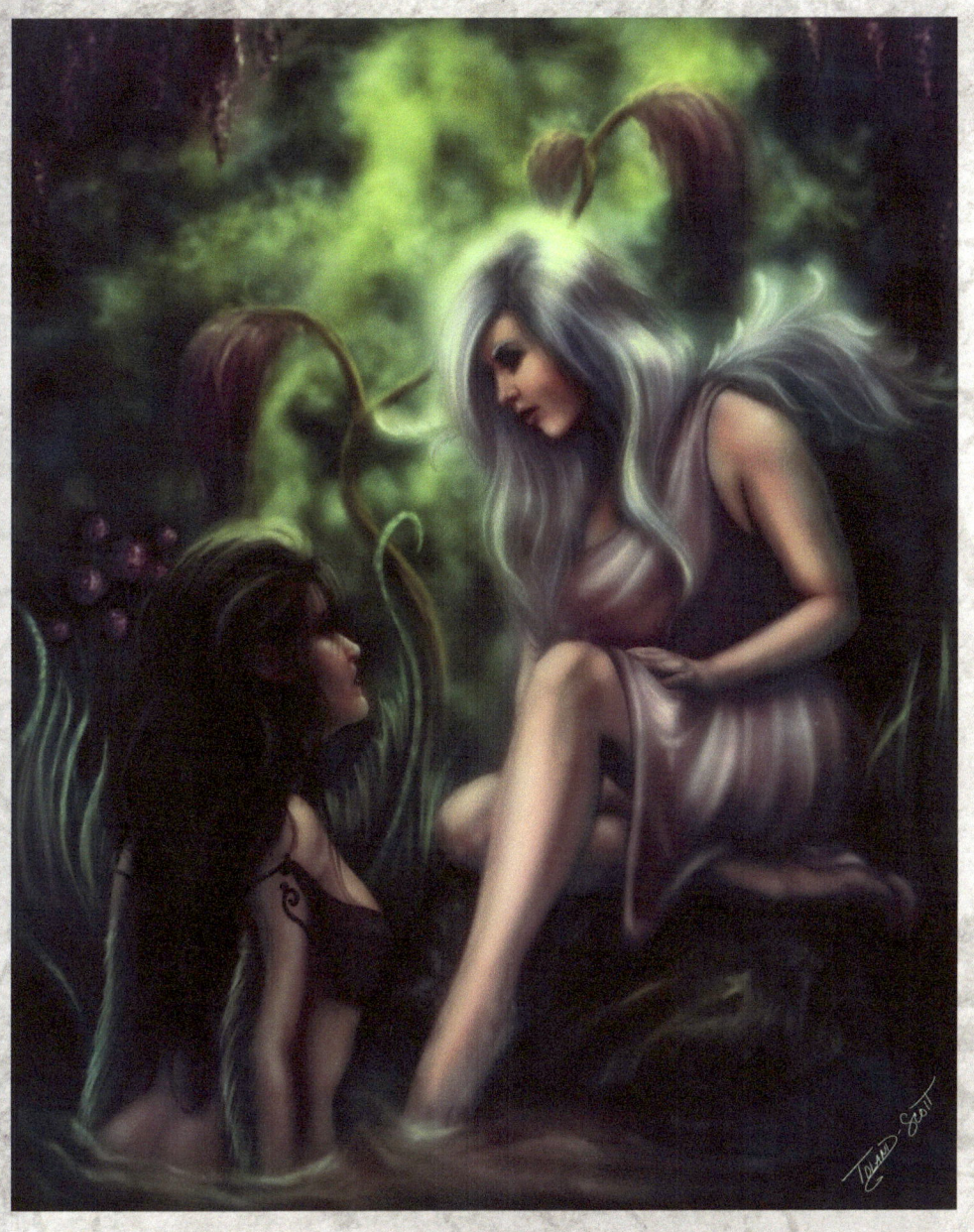

WORLDS APART - These two are as surprised to see one another as you would be to see one of them. They represent Separation in the oracle deck.

This was painted digitally in 2013.

Tiffany Toland-Scott lives near the capitol of Montana with her husband, son, and a menagerie of pets. She paints and publishes a variety of products full-time from her home studio and workshop.

Tiffany's work can be found online at tiffanysrealm.com and can be purchased in a variety of formats including prints, originals, gift items, books, oracle decks, calendars and more.

Tiffany paints primarily fantasy and Gothic subjects inspired by mythology and folktales. She paints the majority of her work digitally using a large digital tablet and stylus which allows her to paint right on the screen. It is a process similar to traditional painting without the mess and hazard of paint.

All of the works in this book were created digitally.

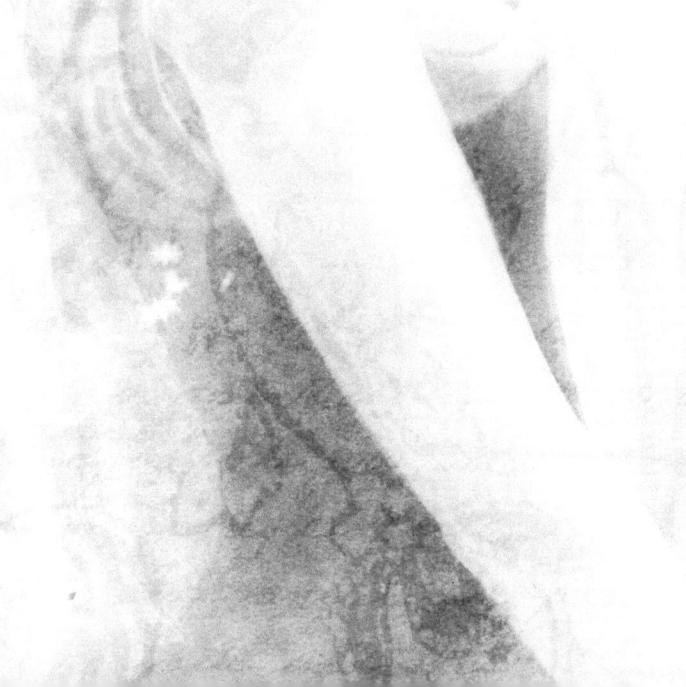

This book and the oracle deck the work comes from was made possible by those generous individuals who contributed to our Kickstarter campaign.

Thank you.

www.ingramcontent.com/pod-product-compliance
Lightning Source LLC
Chambersburg PA
CBHW040923180526
45159CB00002BA/591